PRAISE FOR ALL RISE

"I just finished *All Rise*. The fact that I read it in one day at one setting tells you all you need to know about how riveting it was." – Mike Beebe, former Arkansas governor (2007-2015)

"When his second-grade teacher in Virginia asked Bob Brown what he wanted to be when he grew up, the future Arkansas Supreme Court Justice responded, 'a good man.' With his nicely paced memoir, Brown lays out a strong case that he indeed achieved his aspiration – and much more." – Nate Coulter, executive director, Central Arkansas Library System

"If Bob Brown had not chosen a career in law and had a distinguished record as a jurist on the Arkansas Supreme Court, writing a number of its significant decisions, he could have excelled even more as an author. For those interested in a perceptive view of Arkansas history in recent decades, this book is a very good read." – Walter E. Hussman, Jr., chairman, WEHCO Media

"Bob Brown served our state well on the court and, in this memoir, he recounts his preparation for those years and his tenure dressed in the robes of justice with insight that entertains and informs any and all who are interested in politics or the law." – Archie Schaffer III, consultant, Tyson Foods and Tyson Family Foundation"copy." – Archie Schaffer III, consultant, Tyson Foods and Tyson Family Foundation

"Robert Brown's *All Rise* is a highly enjoyable and entertaining memoir that will appeal to anyone who has spent (or is thinking about spending) time in politics or the law. I couldn't put it down. While I couldn't relate to the legal side of his story as much as the political, he presents the information in a way that a legal neophyte such as myself could understand his career on the bench and appreciate the significance of the opinions he authored." – Will Rockefeller, vice president, Winrock Farms

"In this memoir by the son of a Bishop (SOB) and retired Arkansas Supreme Court Justice, my friend and colleague, a self-professed introvert, opens the door to the inner sanctum: private reflections on his experiences (1) as a white teenager during Little Rock's 1957 Central High desegregation crisis; (2) as an active participant and observer of Arkansas politics; and (3) as an Arkansas Supreme Court Justice — a treasure trove for Arkansas historians!" – Annabelle Tuck, retired Arkansas Supreme Court Justice

ALL RISE

ALL RISE

How Race, Religion, and Politics Shaped My Career on the Arkansas Supreme Court

RETIRED JUSTICE ROBERT L. BROWN

Johnswood Press

About the Cover: The illustration on the cover is a reproduction of The Robing Room, a painting by Dennis McCann that offers a unique look at the day-to-day lives of justices. The justices portrayed are (left to right) Robert Brown, WH "Dub" Arnold (Chief Justice), Don Corbin, Ray Thornton, Lavinski Smith, Tom Glaze, and Annabelle Tuck.

First Printing, 2022

Dedicated to my beloved wife, Charlotte, who weathered the storms and offered guidance, love, and commitment along the way.

The author: "You know, Mr. Stephens, politics is the best game in town."

W.R. "Witt" Stephens: "No, Bob. It's the only game."

CONTENTS

FOREWORD

In this instructive book, my longtime friend Robert L. Brown, one of the most influential justices ever to sit on the Supreme Court of Arkansas, has produced a most appealing personal and professional autobiography.

Brown limns the main outlines of his life, including his family, upbringing, and marriage, and draws on his many years in state and national government to describe his deep involvement in Arkansas's political life. Along the way, he does not forget to relate some revealing anecdotes about the most prominent Arkansas politicians of the last sixty years.

Best of all, the book is written in an actual, clear-headed English, making for a rare respite from the labored efforts sometimes evident in this genre. This is unsurprising, given Brown's liberal arts education and the eloquence of his previous work. Even the parts of the book that discuss his important contributions to Arkansas jurisprudence profit from Brown's determination to avoid jargon and so they speak with clarity and precision to the generally educated reader.

Anyone interested in law, politics, and public policy will profit from reading the book.

– Morris "Buzz" Arnold, senior judge, U.S. Court of Appeals, Eighth Circuit

PREFACE

"I am a part of all that I have met," proclaimed Tennyson's Ulysses. And so it is with most of us. We begin with our genetic makeup of course, but then our adventures, our education, our families, our occupation, and countless other experiences, all feed into the mix and make us who we are.

As you'll see in the pages to come, that's certainly been true of me.

This book tells my story as a preacher's kid and then an SOB (son of a bishop) and how I navigated the Jim Crow South, changed schools six consecutive years (not by choice), weathered the sixties, turned to a career in law, writing, politics, and politics that culminated in my Arkansas Supreme Court judgeship. It is remarkable in that my career was not planned at an early age. I was not a Bill Clinton with a rolodex of important people who could help me along my path. Rather, I was more swept along by events – one leading to another – that ultimately formed my journey.

My father, first as an Episcopal minister and then bishop, was influential in the civil rights movement and wrote about it and spoke out on the issue, which, no doubt, impacted me greatly. This meant that I was not interested in just being a lawyer. I wanted to do more than just practice law or teach law.

All Rise offers a blueprint on how to transition from a liberal arts major to a dispenser of justice. It seems trite to say that I describe how I took advantage of opportunities. Working as a deputy prosecuting attorney and then administrative assistant for Congressman Jim Guy Tucker and then as legal aide and legislative assistant for Governor and Senator Dale Bumpers were huge career leaps for me. They took me out of myself and pushed me – a borderline introvert – into a life of action where I had a voice on some of the major issues of the day.

Asking questions of our leaders and analyzing their careers led me to writing profiles about their lives for various publications, and, fascinated with that information and my personal experience with political figures, I entered the arena of statewide politics and then legal decision making.

My book is more than a "you can do it too" memoir, although there is some of that. It is more a story of how I became a supreme court justice and what I did when I got there. I tell about Little Rock grande dame Aldolphine Terry, who advised me during my younger years to try everything. I took her advice, and with the resulting reservoir of experience, I was able to set aside my reserve and put on a theatrical mask to become Bob Brown "The Candidate" and Bob Brown "The Justice." And with the exceptional help of my wonderful wife, Charlotte, I succeeded.

The book is really about those experiences and my maturation and evolution on issues like equal rights, whether in the civil or criminal forums. Deciding what is fair became my mission and should be the mission for anyone drawn to the justice system. Most importantly, I give examples in *All Rise* of my significant, far-reaching decisions and the articles I have written to improve the judiciary.

My thought is that this book can be a template for anyone flirting with a life on the bench or wanting to know more about the judiciary, including how to get there by election and what awaits you once you arrive.

CHAPTER 1

Texas Beginnings

Texas has always been in my blood.

Born the son of an Episcopal clergyman, I was destined to be a rolling stone, moving from Texas to Virginia and eventually to Arkansas. After my birth in Houston in 1941, the family moved almost immediately to Waco, where my father became rector of the city's only Episcopal church at the time – St. Paul's.

Waco was where we lived during the war years.

My father, Robert R. Brown, was exempt from military service as a minister with two children, but he always contended that comforting parishioners with sons in the military, especially with some inevitable deaths, was almost as wrenching as combat. He was raised in San Antonio and went to Virginia Theological Seminary, an Episcopal seminary in Alexandria, Virginia. His ambition was to be a football coach and work in theology with his coaching.

My mother, Warwick Rust Brown, was from Fairfax, Virginia. She had just graduated from Sweet Briar College and was teaching in an all-girls' school, St. Agnes, close to the seminary, when she first saw my father racing across the seminary campus giving a Texas yell. She never looked back. It was right out of Edna Ferber's *Giant*.

My family was not spared the tragedy of war. The plane of Ellis Middleton, who was married to my mother's sister, Anne Hooe Rust, was shot down over Germany in 1945, and he was killed. My father's brother, Joe Brown, was an Army chaplain in the Italian campaign that scarred him in ways he rarely discussed. He brought me his battered iron helmet and red flashlight as mementos, which I later foolishly traded away. My mother's brother, Johnny Rust, was a naval officer in the Pacific theater.

Even in my early years, I recognized my father as a commanding force who brooked little nonsense from others. He was more military by upbringing, having graduated from the Texas Military Institute before college. His father, my grandfather, had flown biplanes at Kelly Field in San Antonio. Once I remember dad sparring, using my small boxing gloves which covered only half his hands, with Nicky Russell's father in our living room. It was playful at first but then turned semi-serious. It stopped after a few light blows were landed. But Dad also relaxed by regularly playing the piano (the musical version of the Kipling poem "Danny Deever" and "St. Louis Blues") and by wrestling on the floor with me and my older sister, Wickie, while offering us the challenge, *Can you touch my nose?*

My mother, on the other hand, ran the house with the Latino help, but she was more of a gentle soul who also played the piano. On Sunday evenings when Dad was away at nearby missions, she would play and sing hymns, including mournful songs like "Now the Day Is Over."

I later learned that Dad began his ministry in Harlingen, Texas, in the Rio Grande Valley during the Depression (where Wickie was born) because the bishop thought it would be a good place for Dad to learn humility. It was a meager existence for the young minister and his family. For mother, it was a far cry from Fairfax, Virginia, but Dad was too proud to accept financial help from my grandfather, John Rust.

The war years in Waco were a tense time. Food was rationed, and we all planted victory gardens and studied the war pictures in *Life* magazine. And even at the age of six, I knew the families who had a son engaged in combat or a daughter who was working in the war effort.

At the end of 1943, there was a new addition to our family, my sister Kathy. Risktaker that he was, Dad decided to sneak up the back stairs to mother's hospital room after the birth with me in tow. We caught a glimpse of mother, who was flat on her back, still drugged from the ether. We waved to the passive figure who barely responded. She would not come home for a week. It was all very perplexing to me. I just knew that I wanted mother to come home.

Sanger Avenue Elementary was my first school, but I spent much of my first six years participating in neighborhood gangs like the Coyote Kids, organized by Wickie, who was a tomboy and a born leader. She was three years older than me and always loyal and my fierce defender. Because of her creativity and gift for adventure, I quickly fell into the role of her devoted follower.

I had multiple fights with my new friend, Nicky Russell, in the field between our houses, and tried to avoid scorpions, tarantulas, rats, snakes, garbage pickers, and bands of "gypsies" who, on occasion, came to town. Lessons were learned. Grabbing a bumble-bee thinking it was a butterfly provided an early one.

I would also wander down the street to the Chateau on Chateau Drive where my first girlfriend lived. Occasionally, on the weekends, my dad and I would go to a neighboring ranch and ride horses. Sliding off one due to a weak cinch is etched in my memory. But unlike Rock Hudson's son in *Giant*, I liked riding.

In our backyard we had pecan and wild cherry trees and could eat our fill. We had one or two dust storms during this time that I remember causing my mother to panic and seal the windows with tape. It did not completely work. And it was hot. Beastly hot. It was a pure Texas existence.

All that changed with my father's call to a church in Richmond, Virginia (Photograph 1).

CHAPTER 2

Richmond

Dad would become the rector of St. Paul's Episcopal Church in Richmond, which was a plum assignment.

Richmond was the polar opposite of Waco. It was more refined and cosmopolitan compared to the mesquite and cattle culture of Texas that I was used to. My first few nights in Richmond, Dad and I stayed in the dark and somewhat eerie downtown home of a St. Paul parishioner. The parishioner's daughter, who was my age, dressed in heavy velvet dresses and wore lace collars. This stood in stark contrast to the less formal attire of the Waco cowgirls.

St. Paul's was directly across from the historic Virginia State Capitol, which was designed by Thomas Jefferson. It had been the church of Robert E. Lee and Jefferson Davis during the Civil War and now claimed many of the first families of Virginia as communicants.

A mosaic of Leonardo da Vinci's *The Last Supper* served as the backdrop behind the church's altar, and the stained-glass windows surrounding the nave were all treasures, including the Lee Window, which depicted Moses casting aside the Egyptian scepter offered to him by the Pharaoh so he could serve his own people, the Israelites. To passionate Southerners, it was Lee's story, as well, when he chose to fight for the South after being offered a major command in the North.

A few blocks away, Monument Avenue boasted the statues of confederate generals Robert E. Lee, Stonewall Jackson, and J.E.B. Stuart. More recently, tennis great Arthur Ashe was added to the group. (The statue of Robert E. Lee was recently removed as not being in sync with the times.)

When Dad first arrived at St. Paul's, an elderly woman asked him, "Have you seen the General?" or "How is the General?" It evolved that as a girl she had ridden on a general's knee. Then it dawned on Dad that the General she referred to was Lee. Doing the math, it had been eighty-two years since the end of the Civil War. For a woman in her early nineties, the story was entirely plausible. The Civil War was still very much upon us.

In 1948, while my father was in his second year at St. Paul's, a drunken sailor broke into the church on a Saturday night and wreaked havoc. He smashed his fist through priceless windows, including the Lee Window, and was cut and bruised in the process. We could see his blood in the hallways the next morning when we went to Sunday School. The congregation was outraged, but my father immediately came to his rescue. He publicly forgave the sailor, which was citywide news. Even my second-grade teacher, Mrs. Worthington, mentioned it in class and praised his compassion. I was proud, because Dad was famous and had apparently done the right thing in forgiving the sailor. I knew, even at the age of seven, that his act of forgiveness was courageous.

The same Mrs. Worthington polled our second form (grade) class on what we wanted to be when we grew up. I dutifully responded, "A good man," not realizing that the question was focused more on a favored profession like doctor, minister, or lawyer. Needless to say, her heart melted, and she called my parents. I still believe my answer was the correct one.

I attended St. Christopher's, a private Christian boy's school in Richmond, and my education there, particularly in the Lower School, was Victorian bred. We learned to spell from *The Calvert Speller* in the second form, the multiplication tables in the third form, and the Roman emperors in the fifth.

Our two school teams, forever in competition, were the Lees and the Jacksons. I was a Jackson. We fought it out on the playing fields but also in Declamation Contests, where we recited poems, en masse or individually, like Macaulay's "Horatius at the Bridge," McCrae's "In Flander's Fields," Magee's "High Flight," and Kipling's "If," for points. Later, in a memorable faceoff for the senior class, one finalist chose Poe's "The Raven," and the other chose Marc Antony's funeral oration from *Julius Caesar*. The Antony orator won, in part because he wore a toga sprinkled with catsup to simulate Caesar's blood. I thought his performance was riveting, but those less enamored of his theatrics found it pretentious and nerdy.

Accidents plagued me in elementary school. In the third form, I walked into a baseball bat swung by classmate Birdie Davenport. My nose was crushed, but never diagnosed as broken. The following year another classmate, Billy King, who would later excel as an all-star quarterback at Dartmouth College, threw me down on the concrete surface of our gym and cracked my two front teeth. (The same Billy King would appear before my court decades later as counsel for Ford Motor Company. More on that later.) Bloody noses were a regular occurrence for me in football, which we began playing in pads at age seven.

Accidents notwithstanding, the late forties and early fifties in Richmond were a privileged time for me. My friends and I roamed the city freely on bicycles and by city bus without fear, and we played chase in the remains of the federal trenches that surrounded Richmond during the Civil War in the adjoining neighborhood called Windsor Farms.

My best friend and running mate, Leslie Cheek, was the grandson of Robert E. Lee biographer, Douglas Southall Freeman, whom we joined for tea one Sunday afternoon. My dad, who was a Civil War buff, told me I would always remember that experience, but I was doubtful. It was merely a meeting with an old man who was polite and a gentleman but hardly dynamic to a ten-year-old.

Leslie's father, Leslie Cheek, Jr., was director of the Virginia Museum of Fine Arts, and his mother, Mary Tyler Freeman Cheek, was a surrogate mother to me. She had gone to Vassar College and was very progressive for Richmond. I would join the Cheek family for visits to their farm near Lake Lure, North Carolina, and down to the art museum to try on medieval armor. They were an exceedingly creative and entertaining family. At Lake Lure, Leslie and I would milk the cows and slop the hogs. We would aquaplane on the lake and then the family and guests would put on skits for prizes. At times, we were asked what we thought about the Korean War and President Harry Truman. We admitted that we knew that America was fighting the communists in Korea but little else.

Political discussions were not the norm around our dining room table, but it was clear that President Truman was not a favorite of my parents. I am not certain whether it was the Hawaiian shirts, the owl-like glasses, or the wide grin that alienated them. Or it may have been his policies. My mother, in particular, found him crass. Truman's unpopularity was so pronounced that I was incredulous when told in 1949 that a couple who had voted for Truman were coming over to play bridge with my parents. Who could these freaks be? So I snuck down the stairs to get a glimpse of this decidedly odd couple. To my surprise, they looked perfectly normal.

Truman's unpopularity crescendoed with the firing of General Douglas MacArthur for disobedience during the Korean War. It was 1951, and everyone in my bubble opposed the decision. When Mac-Arthur was asked to address the joint session of Congress after he returned from Korea following his dismissal, my fourth form class was told it was too important to miss. We were taken to a neighbor's house to watch the "Old Soldiers Never Die" speech. Afterward, we could all quote at least some of the lines:

"Old soldiers never die, they just fade away."

And like the old soldier of that ballad, I now close my military career and just fade away—an old soldier who tried to do his duty as God gave him the light to see that duty.

Good-bye.

MacArthur was deified in Richmond. Most of my generation liked him because he had the scrambled eggs on his cap, wore dark glasses, and smoked a corncob pipe. With his jutting jaw, he was every inch a stud. Plus, we had all become engrossed in *Victory at Sea* on weekend television about the war in the Pacific, where MacArthur's exploits loomed large.

It was only much later that I realized what a great president Harry Truman had been. Arkansas Governor Dale Bumpers underscored this when he told me about his visit to Independence, Missouri in 1971 to talk with the retired president. Bumpers had just been elected governor in 1970 and was somewhat frustrated as he learned about the job. He whined to the thirty-third president of the United States about how difficult it was to deal with the Arkansas legislature on budget matters and the prison system. Then, it suddenly dawned on him that here sat the man who had negotiated peace for Europe at the Potsdam Conference with Churchill and Stalin, made the decision to drop the atomic bombs on Japan, and fired MacArthur. Bumpers suddenly felt humbled and chagrined.

Truman turned to him and offered lasting advice: "Always be honest with the people, Dale. They can handle the truth." According to Bumpers, he had never liked Truman much until he fired MacArthur, who he considered a pompous ass and a dangerous demagogue. Firing MacArthur was an act of "great courage," Bumpers would later say.

By 1952, my political enthusiasm for MacArthur had waned, only to be replaced by my allegiance to another five-star general – Dwight D. Eisenhower ("Ike"). That summer, the Republican National Convention was broadcast live on television from Chicago, and Wickie and I watched the nip and tuck roll call votes for the nomination. We were not impartial. We were solidly in the Ike camp and were exhilarated as he inched slowly ahead of the dour Robert Taft.

After he won the nomination, Eisenhower came to Richmond in September 1952 during his presidential campaign against Democrat Adlai Stevenson. Unfairly cast as weak and an egghead, and severely deficient in the personality quotient, Stevenson was no match for the general with the sunburst smile. Richmond, a final stop on the day's whistle-stop tour, was ecstatic and decked out in bunting and flags to greet the general. Spotlights and music accompanied his entry at night. It was like a triumphant Roman general returning from war, and we were all transfixed citizens. The chants "I like Ike" were a steady drumbeat, and you could feel the crack in the Democrat Party's Solid South, as Virginia began to pull away.

Later, my mother-in-law, Anne Banks, would claim that Eisenhower's campaign had borrowed the slogan "I like Ike" from Ike Murry, who used it in his unsuccessful gubernatorial bid earlier in Arkansas in 1952. Anne proudly announced that the slogan was her idea, and that she had shared it with her good friend, Murry.

That was only the beginning of my contact with Ike through my family. My father, with the help of Assistant Secretary of State Walter Robinson, who was a parishioner, invited Eisenhower to Sunday services at St. Paul's Church on May 9, 1954. It was Mother's Day, and Ike and Mamie made the pilgrimage. The city was in awe once more. Virginia's voluntary militia, the Richmond Blues, marched in celebration with Governor William Battle. As a Boy Scout, I was part of the honor guard to welcome him (Photograph 2). If I could have voted, there is no doubt I would have cast my vote for the Republican general.

And yet, voting for Eisenhower would have been something akin to treason in some quarters of my family. My maternal grandfather, John Warwick Rust, lived in Fairfax, Virginia, and was prominent in the anti-Republican camp. Family lore had it that he had come to Fairfax from the Shenandoah Valley as a young man at the turn of the twentieth century with $20 in his pocket. His confederate credentials were rock solid. His father, Captain John Rust, rode with General Turner Ashby's cavalry, known as the Mountain Rangers, in the Civil War. According to family history, Captain Rust had five horses shot out from under him.

Like many unreconstructed confederates, my grandfather refused to reconcile and championed the Lost Cause. He also kept a bowl on his bureau to store his pennies because he refused to spend a coin with Lincoln's image on it. Putting on my smart aleck hat, I would taunt him from time to time and ask him what he thought of Abraham Lincoln.

"He was a bad man, Bobby," would come his answer. "A bad man."

My grandfather always repeated things.

Despite his bitterness about the Civil War and its aftermath, my grandfather prospered as a lawyer, farmer, landowner, and banker in Fairfax and Falls Church, and he served two terms in the Virginia State Senate. As such, he was part of the Byrd Machine, the highly effective Democratic organization led by United States Senator Harry Byrd. One of the reasons Virginia broke with the Solid South in 1952 was that Byrd signaled, by his silence, that it was permissible for Virginians to vote for Ike.

Granddaddy Rust's white stucco-on-brick house in Fairfax stood on a hill overlooking Chain Bridge Road. My mother, Warwick Rust Brown, was born in the house. It was surrounded by fourteen acres of fields and abutted the Fairfax County Courthouse. On one of those acres, my grandfather had planted a vegetable garden that he hand-plowed every afternoon as an alternative to having cocktails. With fresh tomatoes, corn, and beans, accompanied by cured Virginia hams from the smokehouse, dining in Fairfax as a young boy was a culinary delight. It was also a riot. We would sit outside at picnic tables and my mother's sister, Anne Hooe, and brother, Johnny, would tease and cut up. It was wonderful.

There were also the Civil War artifacts the garden produced. The field between my grandfather's house and the courthouse was where the federal troops had bivouacked at the end of the Civil War. Because of that, belt buckles, midi balls, masonry shells, bayonets, and even muskets were routinely uncovered. There was a makeshift museum on the property for what was collected. Wickie and I took some of these treasures back to Richmond to store in our treasure boxes. Later in Little Rock, my friend Griffin Smith tried to outbargain my sister Wickie for her coin collection and artifacts. He was not successful.

Young and naïve though my peer group was in the early to mid-fifties, we knew the decade following World War II was a pivotal time for America. Hitler and Hirohito may have been defeated, but the Soviet Union and the spread of communism were now the global threats. President Truman had committed troops through NATO to defend

South Korea, and hydrogen bomb tests in Yucca Flats, Nevada, were being shown to the nation on morning television. About this time, to my great surprise, my parents bought me a World War II humped back Cushman motor scooter, which could reach an impressive 35 miles per hour. My stock among my peers soared. The balance of power in my neighborhood had clearly shifted.

Then there was Wisconsin Senator Joe McCarthy and the Red Scare. McCarthy railed so much against communist infiltration into our government that he eventually became a caricature of himself. Suddenly, he was a joke in my Boy Scouts troop, and we would lampoon his antics in the televised Army-McCarthy hearings. "Mr. Chairman, Mr. Chairman, I have in my hand a list of one-hundred twenty-three communists in the State Department," we would mimic. I do not know who first said this, but Dale Bumpers, Arkansas Governor (1971-75) and United States Senator (1975-1999), often repeated it: "Once you become a joke and you are laughed at, you are on the downhill side of your political career." So it was with McCarthy.

As a young boy, my news first came from John Cameron Swayze and his fifteen-minute telecast and, of course, *Life* magazine. Because of *Life*, I knew about Martin Luther King, Jr., and his successful "back of the bus" boycott in Montgomery, Alabama. We had also read the stories of Emmett Till, who was horribly lynched in Mississippi for whistling at a white woman. My friend, Justice Andree Roaf, who was African American and served on the Supreme Court with me, later said she had seen a photograph of the bloated and battered face of Till in his coffin, and it still haunted her. And we were aware that racial integration of the public schools – not St. Christopher's – was coming fast, somehow, some way, but we were not well versed in the intricacies of the two Supreme Court decisions in *Brown v. Board of Education*. In group discussions, opinions ranged from the segregationists among us saying, "Send the Blacks back to Africa," to the braver of us saying simply that we favored integration. The fact that Blacks had inferior schools and were still subjected to arcane Jim Crow laws was not lost on me.

One evening when I was going home by city bus from a Boy Scouts meeting at St. Paul's, an African American man refused to go to the back of the bus as the bus driver ordered. The bus driver immediately pulled to the side of the street and stopped the bus.

"I'm not moving till you get to the back of the bus," he snarled. There was a fearful silence among the other passengers, Black and white, and the African American man, seated near the front, did not budge. After about five minutes that seemed an eternity, he stood up and crouched in the aisle: "I want your license number," he said to the driver, looking at the front window where it was posted, and wrote it down. The driver, clearly irritated, opened the side door, and the man exited. He then pulled away from the curb in a jerky motion and drove on. I sat in stunned silence, knowing that the Black man was right. This was Rosa Parks all over again. The times, they were clearly "a changin'," although certainly not fast enough.

During my eight years in Richmond (1947 to 1955), and in Texas before that, I had lived a segregated, separate-but-equal, Jim Crow existence. We had had Black single women either live with us as domestic servants or come to our house on a daily basis. But I rarely intermingled with my Black peers.

When I was about ten and attending a friend's birthday party in the country outside of Richmond, I got hopelessly lost when I went back in the woods to retrieve my golden cap pistol following the party. As I wandered deeper and deeper into unknown territory, I heard a voice call out, like a mother calling her son to come home. Following the voice, I soon came upon an African American family and their humble house and surroundings. I explained what had happened to me and named the family who were my hosts. The mother directed her son to take me to the home. We walked for about thirty minutes, with my guide walking about ten feet in front of me and neither of us saying a word. That night when I thought about it, I got emotional about the gulf between the races. I had been returned to safety by an unknown contemporary who lived in a different, segregated world and under much harsher conditions.

There was tension in the air in the mid-1950s. Everyone seemed on edge when it came to the "Race Issue." Where previously events like the Harlem Globetrotters coming to town and playing a bumbling all-white team (the Washington Generals) were harmless and fun-filled, now they generated racial slurs from the whites in the crowd. Something clearly was about to blow.

Amidst it all, my father was fast becoming an important figure within the Episcopal Church. In the late 1940s, he was editor of the *Southern Churchman*, which discussed the church and race relations. He wrote two books, *Miracle of the Cross* on Christ's seven last words, and *Friendly Enemies*, which was a compilation of sermons on forgiveness. In 1948, he went to Germany to work with people who were displaced because of the war. He was a comer and definitely on track to become bishop.

Dad's sermons were performances. He peppered them with poignant illustrations, stories, and quotations to bring home his points. And they were brilliantly done. Favorite authors were T.S. Eliot and George Bernard Shaw, whom he quoted unsparingly. He was a commanding presence, both in the pulpit and out in the community. Challenges to his authority were rare. I learned quickly to tiptoe around his moods and above all else not to be a source of embarrassment for him. On the latter point, I was not altogether successful.

For my part, I was a B-plus student in the throes of adolescence with all that entails. The bolder of us began dating seriously, but we all went to parties to dance in the dark to slow "Your Hit Parade" songs with the girls from St. Catherine's School.

Then a bomb fell. My dad announced he had been elected bishop of Arkansas, and we were all moving to Little Rock.

CHAPTER 3

Little Rock

"You're moving where?" my Richmond friend, Dickie Wilson, asked.

"Arkansas," I said matter-of-factly.

"So, you'll be rolling the sand, not mowing the grass?"

We both laughed a bit uncomfortably. There was no doubt my friend saw me as abandoning culture for life in the Wild West, much like the Saturday afternoon cowboy movies we did not miss. I knew that was wrong, but how wrong I was not certain (Photograph 3).

My father had indeed been elected the Episcopal Bishop of Arkansas, which caused the move in August 1955. He would actually serve for a year as bishop coadjutor, which was an assistant bishop to the diocesan bishop, R. Bland Mitchell. When Dad's election was announced on Richmond radio, one reporter said he would be the "Bishop Co-Agitator" of Arkansas. As it turned out, given Dad's role in the coming Central High desegregation crisis, co-agitator would not be far off the mark in the minds of some.

It was mid-morning that August when my father and I crossed the Mississippi River into Arkansas. We were the first car; my mother and two sisters were in the second. Driving all night in a two-car caravan had been a new and exhausting experience, and we were groggy and irritable. My parents, Wickie, and I shared the driving chore, but because

I had just been licensed in Virginia to drive with an adult and was only fourteen, my shifts were limited.

We were beginning a new life, which was exciting yet daunting at the same time. Driving through Memphis before the interstate highway system had been built was irksome. Traffic was heavy in the early morning hours, and stoplights abounded. Our pair of Chevrolets were not air conditioned, and my father was a pack-a-day Lucky Strike smoker. The tobacco, bumper-to-bumper traffic, and the oppressive heat combined to make my grand entrance into Arkansas akin to passing through the gates of hell. Only crossing the vast Mississippi River salvaged the situation. It was a glorious sight and unlike anything I had ever seen.

Once on the Arkansas side of the river and with Memphis a dim memory, it was my time to drive. The two-lane state Highway 70 was bracketed on each side by murky, brown swamps filled with wild vegetation, tangled vines, scrub bushes, cypress knees, rotting oaks, and an ample supply of water moccasins. The shoulders and abutting hillsides sloped perilously downward on either side to the swamps, which caused me to give full attention to the task at hand. Drive as close as you can to the center of the road, I thought. And pray.

As I white-knuckled my way down the highway, two large trucks passed with open air trailers crammed full of rambunctious, animated, and sparsely clad men.

"Cotton pickers," my father said flatly. "We're in cotton country."

More trucks followed, and the swamps soon gave way to green fields. It was a unique vision for me and a far cry from the brown and yellow tobacco fields I was used to in Virginia.

Our caravan arrived in Little Rock mid-afternoon, and I was taken to the home of Jim Mitchell. He was a year younger than me and soon became a good and lifelong friend. His father, Will Mitchell, was a lawyer and chancellor for the Episcopal Diocese of Arkansas. His sister, Frances, offered to drive Wickie and me around Little Rock my first weekend to show us the sights, which included the new governor's mansion, a red brick structure built in the neoclassical style.

"You'll never guess who lives there," Jim said, turning to me from the front seat. "Orval Faubus," he intoned with a full hillbilly twang. Little did I realize that the man with the cornpone name would soon have a lasting effect on the world's perception of Arkansas and on my future as well. He would be a formidable political force and racial fear monger throughout the South, and he would leave a stain on the state that has yet to be fully removed.

For now, Little Rock was tranquil, and all seemed right in the Jim Crow world.

New friends were quickly made, and I found that many were related by blood, like the Mitchells, the Cockrills, the Grobmyers, the Waits, the Tedfords and so forth. They all lived in a bubble called the Heights – short for the historic Pulaski Heights neighborhood – in proximity to the Country Club of Little Rock. It was much like the Scotts, the Williamses, the Bococks, and the Bryans in Richmond.

Dad was consecrated bishop on October 5, 1955, and it was a grand affair. All the Episcopal clergy attended in vestments. Fifteen bishops from other dioceses came for the laying on of hands. The news coverage was intense, much more so than today for a comparable consecration. I have always maintained that being a bishop's son was not easy, but that the pluses outweighed the minuses. Again, I was proud of what Dad had accomplished. And I was entranced by the lavish ceremony.

I was quickly assimilated into the upper-middle-class culture as the son of the Episcopal bishop and found myself ahead academically in the public schools, particularly in Latin and algebra, in the ninth grade of the newly opened Forest Heights Junior High School. Where I was lacking was in a basic understanding of civics and recent United States history, though I was well versed in Virginia history.

What singled me out from my peer group was my pronounced and distinct Virginia accent. When translating ursa (bear) in my ninth grade Latin class, I said, "Bā-ah." Our Latin teacher, Mrs. Robbins, stopped the class and, dumbfounded, asked, "What did you say?" I repeated my answer, having no idea what the problem was. Henceforth, I was known far and wide as "Bā-ah Brown." A slight Virginia accent still afflicts me to this day.

There was one other problem. While living in Richmond, I had not done much hunting. That would change quickly in Arkansas. My new peer group were all duck, bird (quail), and dove hunters. Nothing would do but that they take me out on a variety of hunts. My first duck hunt, I stood hip deep in water and never took a shot because I wasn't clear on how to reload the shotgun. My quail hunt was more eventful. When the bird dog flushed a covey of quail, I wheeled around to my right to shoot, only to see our guide, who was walking with us in a straight line, hit the ground. When he got up, he said, "Capt'n, don't ever do that again." All I can say is I got better over the years.

Forest Heights was a one-story, ranch style school with no air conditioning. Teenage sweat abounded with the accompanying odor. I went out for football and enjoyed that because I liked to hit. Elvis Presley came to town in early Spring 1956, and the world stood still as rockabilly took hold. At the concert, a classmate, Edith Ax, who was seated behind me, beat on my seat in a frenzy. Then came Little Richard and Carl Perkins. Rock music had never been better.

The following year I entered the iconic Central High School as a sophomore. It was the year before integration, the Little Rock Nine, and the invasion of the 101st Airborne Division sent in by President Eisenhower. This meant it was the last year of segregation in one of the premier high schools in the South.

Apart from a diverse student body, Central High had it all. It was three grades of high school taught in a magnificent building (a mix of Collegiate Gothic and Art Deco) with more than two thousand students. It had a marching band and a football team that went undefeated. It also had a full-blown minstrel show with an interlocutor and four end men in black face sponsored by the Key Club, which no one questioned out loud, and a performance of the football team dressed in tutus. Central's best students peppered the Ivy League schools.

But then the bottom fell out.

Even now, it is difficult to grasp in full the calamity that took shape and enveloped my school, my city, and my state for the next two years. The last two months of my sophomore year at Central High, the word was out that half the students would be attending a new high school, Hall High School, the following year. Black students were to enroll at Central High, but not at Hall High, which was located in what was then considered west Little Rock. This was the more affluent part of the city where the business and professional leaders lived. It was home for the country club set.

In early 1957 Little Rock School Superintendent Virgil Blossom, had supposedly laid the groundwork for integration at Central High with multiple civic club speeches and news releases about the two *Brown* decisions in the United States Supreme Court, but it was not until integration was upon us and nine Black high school students were set to enter Central High in August that the "aginners" rose and began to howl. They had a receptive audience in one primary figure, Governor Orval E. Faubus.

My close friends and I were all engaged in the torture of Hall High's two-a-day football practices in August 1957 and were oblivious to everything but our soreness and fatigue. Yet a few blocks away, a constitutional crisis of immense proportion was congealing with Governor Faubus on one side and the United States Supreme Court and President Eisenhower on the other. That was like a different world to me. Sure, some of my friends at Central High were embroiled in what was going on in the news, like school president Ralph Brodie, who accepted integration and the Supreme Court decisions. My running mates at Hall High for the most part, like Jim Mitchell and Thurston Roach, were also moderate. Public racial epithets, like using the N-word, were considered coarse and bad form.

The issue of who would prevail in the Central High crisis was never really in doubt. Federal law under the United States Constitution was the supreme law of the land, and the Civil War had been fought over that issue. I understood that, as I was certain Governor Faubus did. But

Faubus was going to milk his segregationist stance for all its political worth. And it was worth a considerable amount.

The Central High story is well known. On September 4, 1957, Faubus called out the state militia, which served as the National Guard, to block the entry of the Little Rock Nine into Central High. On September 20, appointed federal Judge Ronald Davies from North Dakota, who assumed the bench after the regular federal judge recused, ordered the National Guard not to interfere with the integration of Central High and to enforce the admission of the nine Black students to Central. Governor Faubus then withdrew the National Guard from Central High.

On September 23, a white mob galvanized and fights broke out, causing the nine students to be whisked away from the school. The next day President Eisenhower ordered the 101st Airborne Division from Kentucky to "occupy" Little Rock and enforce the two *Brown v. Board of Education* desegregation decisions, thus enabling the Little Rock Nine to enter Central High. That is when my father swung into action.

Following the violence on September 23, my father, as the Episcopal bishop, crafted a pastoral letter to all Episcopalians in Little Rock in which he "abhorred" the violence, invoked the Ministry of Reconciliation from Paul's Second Letter to the Corinthians, and endorsed the "brotherhood of man." It was a call for unity and to follow the law.

The letter, in Dad's words, was met with an "uneasy silence" from many of his flock and the segregationist community as well. The business community, in particular, flinched at Dad's stand. The mothers of my friends, however, believed more in what Dad was trying to do. Some confidentially told me that. Again, I was proud of what Dad was doing and believed as bishop he should take a stand in favor of our common humanity.

Undaunted, Dad next led a group of clergy, rabbis, and ministers, including Rabbi Ira Sanders, Roman Catholic Bishop Albert L. Fletcher, Methodist Bishop Paul Martin, Monsignor O'Connell, Dr. W.O. Vaught, and Rev. Dunbar Ogden, in calling for a Day of Prayer to be held on October 12 – Columbus Day – to pray for God's help in resolving the crisis. President Eisenhower and Governor Faubus both wrote letters endorsing the Day of Prayer, and, as church bells rang, eight to ten thousand citizens flocked to Little Rock churches and synagogues to pray for their city (Photograph 4).

The Day of Prayer received national and international acclaim and media attention. But there were dissenters like a group known as the Central High Mothers who published an advertisement in a local newspaper objecting to ministers fostering "race mixing" in the public schools.

A seismic split had divided Little Rock primarily along racial lines, but not entirely. Progressive whites and the editor of the editorial page for the *Arkansas Gazette*, Harry Ashmore, argued that Little Rock must abide by the law of the land regardless of personal views. This meant the two *Brown* decisions. My father fell into this category of obedience. It meant he had some quiet support from Episcopal parishioners, but it was offset by an abundance of old friends who had supported him for bishop and befriended him when he came to Little Rock, but who now opposed desegregation and crossed the street to avoid greeting him.

That was all in stark contrast to the favorable national press he received in *Time* and *Life* magazines and the *Living Church* for his principled stand and in some of the local press as well. When President Eisenhower asked him to Washington to talk about bettering the Little Rock situation, he was dubbed "The Mystery Bishop" by the press. Even close friends of my parents believed Dad was becoming too much of an activist on civil rights. On the home front, harassing telephone calls afflicted my mother, and she learned to keep a whistle nearby to answer the sometimes-silent callers with a shrill response. It was a traumatic time.

But for me as a junior at the newly commissioned Hall High School, life was pretty normal. We heard the stories of old friends being involved in incidents with the Black students at Central High, like pushing and dumping chili in their laps at lunch, but that seemed to us another world.

For my part, I was a full-blown teenager and something of a wise ass. The girl I loved had fallen for another, and the novelty of the bishop's boy from Virginia had worn off. I had lettered in football, and the coach, Ray Peters, called me "muscles," which was far from the truth. But like most of my peers, I was at loose ends.

And my prowess in the classroom was less than admirable. I was now a solid B student and a cut-up in class. And yet one class did appeal – American Literature – taught by Nancy Popperfuss. She made it come alive through *Moby Dick, Huckleberry Finn,* Walt Whitman, and *The Scarlett Letter.* She nurtured a spark that would stay lit for another seven years.

One evening, however, stood out for me. While I was attending Hall High, I was asked to meet at night with several Quaker leaders who had come to Little Rock to try to soothe the racial tension and a couple of the Little Rock Nine to talk about the problems at Central High. Undoubtedly, my father's leadership in the crisis was the reason I was invited.

I remember the Quaker leader first calling for prayer. Melba Patillo, one of the Little Rock Nine, was with us. At one point, the issue of whether the Nine felt inferior academically or socially to the white students was raised. Melba answered in a strong and emphatic voice: "I don't feel inferior to anybody." I believed her and was surprised by her confidence and boldness, though I should not have been. That encounter for me was rare. Before then, I had had no contact with the Little Rock Nine.

In 1958, my father published a book about the Little Rock crisis, *Bigger Than Little Rock.* Close friends, again, had advised him not to write it because it was seen as too "liberal." He disagreed and forged ahead. The book was a relatively short account of the role of the Little Rock churches and synagogues in attempting to heal the schism in Little Rock caused by the two *Brown* decisions and Governor Faubus. It received international acclaim. No less a person than Alan Paton praised the book for using prayer to offer a solution to entrenched racism. Paton had written similarly about apartheid in South Africa in *Cry, the Beloved Country*.

That summer of 1958 I had been farmed out to Kanuga, an Episcopal church center outside of Hendersonville, North Carolina, because my parents would be at the Lambeth Conference in London, England, for Anglican and Episcopalian bishops. Kanuga was open to vacationing families who would enjoy recreation in the Blue Ridge mountains, as well as young campers.

My task at Kanuga was to be one of the lifeguards for church campers and the visiting families. The swimming area was a roped-off part of a spring-filled lake with diving boards and a large wooden floating raft on the north edge. A pavilion for dances, basketball, and staff plays bordered the south end. Social life among the staff was brimfull. There was much campfire spooning and singing. Songs from The Weavers at Carnegie Hall and the Kingston Trio were favorites. For me, Kanuga put a bow on the Eisenhower Fifties.

It was there I realized the scope and significance of what had happened at Central High with the Little Rock Nine the previous year. Everyone knew about it at Kanuga, visitors and staff alike. The kitchen staff was Black and good guys. They did not comment openly about Central High, nor did we, but we would play them in basketball and tension was palpable. Once we even won.

All of this was prelude to the uprooting that would face me the following school year – my senior year. Fearing violence for the 1958-59 school year after the 101st Airborne Division was removed from Central High, the Little Rock School Board petitioned the federal district court to delay integration for two years. That case, *Cooper v. Aaron*, was eventually heard by the United States Supreme Court in August 1958 right before Central High, Hall High, Dunbar High (an all-Black school), and Little Rock Tech were about to open. The Supreme Court denied the petition to delay. Governor Faubus then closed the high schools for the 1958-59 school year rather than integrate, which the General Assembly had given him the authority to do if voters in the school district supported it. A referendum was taken of Little Rock's registered voters in September 1958, and a vast majority (three-to-one) agreed to close the schools rather than integrate.

Now the question for my family was where would I go to school for my senior year? National news outlets came to student gatherings in Little Rock that September and asked us whether we favored integration. As for me and my peers, though far from political activists we opted for integrated schools and told the press that. It was a no brainer on our part. My aunt, Eleanor Mattern, saw me say that on network television from her home in East Lansing, Michigan. But, as already noted, the vote was overwhelming to close down the schools.

The "Lost Year," as it became known, was tragic for students of both races – more than 3,665 of us lost our opportunity for a public education in Little Rock that year. Many had no place to go to high school and forfeited their diplomas. Others were farmed out to high schools around the state or sent outside the state to relatives' homes or boarding schools. I was lucky. Because of Dad's friendship with the Episcopal bishop of Texas, John Hines, I was given a free senior year education at St. Stephen's Episcopal School in Austin, Texas – a coeducational boarding school. Traveling to Austin with another Little Rock refugee, Howard Cockrill, we embarked on a unique educational experience in the mesquite-covered hills of Texas.

My arrival at St. Stephen's came at least two weeks after school had started. And, of course, Howard and I were curiosities. Some students believed we were there to avoid integration in Little Rock. They were disabused of this when my father's book, *Bigger Than Little Rock*, came out later that fall.

St. Stephen's was a unique experience that really saved me. A coeducational boarding school was not commonplace in 1958 and led to dashes to the girls' dorms after midnight. But the curriculum was rigorous. My preeminence in Little Rock public schools had faded. Trig and solid geometry now loomed as the ultimate tests for me. Football, speeches, the ukulele, which I learned to play at Kanuga, and choir were my salvation. "Cool, Clear Water" by Frankie Laine was my specialty. A girl with the dubious name of Junebug Turner became a favorite.

One thing that didn't change with my move to Texas was that I still wasn't attending an integrated school. Indeed, that would not change until 1963 when I arrived at graduate school at Columbia University in New York City. This meant my social development with other races, and particularly with my Black peers in the South, was stunted. It was a severe deficiency in my formative education.

CHAPTER 4

Sewanee

From a coeducational boarding school, I matriculated into an all-male liberal arts college in 1959. The University of the South is located on the Cumberland Plateau in Sewanee, Tennessee, and as an Episcopal bishop's son, I received a free ride. All Episcopal ministers' sons received the same benefit.

Sewanee, as we call the university, is an Episcopal school owned by twenty-eight Episcopal Dioceses in the South that originally was to open before the Civil War under the leadership of Bishop Leonidas Pope, who was also a Confederate general. While the war stopped that from becoming a reality (the laid cornerstone was destroyed by northern troops), a southern university modeled on Oxford University later rose from the ashes and thrived.

The center of the campus when I arrived in 1959 was All Saints' Chapel, which in reality was a Gothic cathedral. Inside the chapel hung the twenty-eight flags of the owning dioceses dating back in some cases to the founding of the university in 1866. Some flags were old and tattered. In the Oxford mode, professors and top students wore academic gowns.

This Old South legacy of Sewanee was offset in part by Highlander Folk School, six miles away in Monteagle, Tennessee. It was a mecca for budding socialists and communists in the 1930s, and later for civil rights activists. Pete Seeger, Martin Luther King, John Lewis, and Rosa Parks spent time there. So at Sewanee you had the yin of southern conservatism and the yang of the far left influence of the Highlander Folk School just a few miles down the road.

This schizophrenia worried left leaning faculty members at Sewanee to no end. Tom Waring, who was editor of the Charleston, South Carolina, newspaper, *The News and Courier*, was awarded an honorary degree from Sewanee in 1961. The problem was Waring was an avowed segregationist and ardent opponent of the Highlander Folk School. Charleston money was seen as winning out, much to the dismay of Sewanee's more liberal professors, some of whom left Sewanee as a result.

Sewanee was known for many things, not the least of which was its strong literary tradition. The *Sewanee Review*, for instance, was, and still is, one of the country's leading literary quarterlies. Its proximity to Vanderbilt University in Nashville allowed for cross-fertilization decades earlier with the Fugitive poets like Robert Penn Warren and Allen Tate, who were centered there.

On the athletic front, Sewanee went undefeated in 1899 in football, playing twelve teams, including Georgia, Alabama, Ole Miss, Tennessee, and Texas. They almost repeated that feat in 1909, defeating an equal array of southern teams and losing only to Princeton.

And so my college career began, with all that entails. I skated through my freshman year due to my stellar preparation at St. Stephen's and was one of the top two academic performers in my class. The social life occurred primarily in Nashville and Chattanooga and at other schools. And party weekends of course.

During the summer of 1960, I took a job as a volunteer in the west Little Rock office of Joe Hardin, a candidate for governor running against Orval Faubus in the democratic primary. The small staff in the office headed by Dottie Morris knew our cause was just and that Faubus had irrevocably blemished our state with his racial demagoguery. What was ironic about this was that Faubus's father, John Samuel Faubus, was an admitted communist/socialist in Madison County and a champion for equal rights for Blacks. Moreover, Orval, though he swore this was not true in his 1954 successful bid for governor against Francis Cherry, had attended a socialist college, Commonwealth College outside of Mena, Arkansas, which also lauded equal rights for the races. Indeed, Faubus had served as president of the student body.

With this embedded background and practiced sympathy for all races, why would Faubus embrace racial segregation knowing full well that it was contrary to his core beliefs? Harry Ashmore, editorial writer for the *Arkansas Gazette,* probably said it best. Faubus was an opportunist who hungered for a third term as governor in 1958 and the power that accompanied it. Like many political figures before him, he made his pact with the Devil and never looked back.

Four years later, Faubus proved this during a visit with me and a friend from St. Stephen's at his office when he told us that "the n-----" had schools just as good as or better than the whites. "Go see them," he added. Faubus did not recognize me as the son of that "radical" bishop. The reason we got the visit was that the father of my Texas friend had connections with the governor and Faubus was famous. Or infamous.

Hardin really had no chance against Faubus, though he was well connected. Hardin was a successful farmer and had been a state legislator and president of the Farm Bureau. He had also served on the University of Arkansas board of trustees. Despite this, he was a lackluster candidate and, toward the end of his campaign, could not even fill the 2,222 seats at Little Rock's Robinson Auditorium for a state rally. His best asset was his support from Arkansas folksinger Jimmy Driftwood, who had written the "Battle of New Orleans." His second-best asset were the members of the Women's Emergency Committee to Open the Public Schools (WEC), which was founded in 1958 by Adolphine Terry, Vivion Brewer, and Velma Powell, and the list of supporters in Little Rock whom the committee had amassed.

The WEC had about 1,400 members, including my mother, but the group was supposed to have disbanded after the public schools opened in 1959-1960 because it did not want to be viewed as a political arm of the Little Rock liberals. If the WEC help had been known, it would have been additional political fodder for Faubus, who was wont to rail against the Fifth Ward of Little Rock, where many of the wealthy members of the WEC lived.

One of my jobs at the Hardin headquarters was to secretly meet with Vivion Brewer of the WEC and obtain the coveted WEC names for our campaign, which she willingly gave. Those names, though, made little difference when voters headed to the polls on July 26, 1960. Faubus got 58.75 percent of the votes and four times as many as the second-place finisher Hardin. As one columnist put it, all that was left for Hardin after the primary was "a little piece of Driftwood." Faubus then easily defeated Republican Henry Britt in the general election that fall.

After Hardin's severe trouncing, I traveled down to the Lafayette Hotel in Little Rock where the main Hardin campaign headquarters was located. Coming into the office, I spied the principal campaign lieutenants gathered around the desk of the redoubtable Irene Samuel, the campaign manager and key WEC proponent. I would work with Irene later when we both served on the staff of Governor Dale Bumpers in the early 1970s. On this occasion, the conversation centered on why Hardin had lost so miserably. Various theories were espoused, but then Irene broke through the morass. Sitting on the edge of her desk, she said, "Well, I'll tell you one thing. The next time we choose a candidate we're gonna have a committee go visit the wife first." It was a slam at Hardin's wife, Miriam, who clearly had not measured up as an asset in Irene's judgment.

Fourteen years later, on the election night when David Pryor defeated Orval Faubus for governor, Irene would say to Judge Richard Arnold, "I tried for twenty years to beat that son of a bitch and what finally did it was a piece of p----." The reference was to Faubus's attractive new wife, Elizabeth, whom Faubus married after his divorce from Alta. Divorce in Arkansas was still a political liability at that time.

But the Faubus/Hardin race paled in comparison to the battle royal being waged between Republican Richard M. Nixon, Ike's vice president, and Democrat Senator John F. Kennedy. In the fall of 1960 when I was a sophomore at Sewanee, a poll was taken on that race. The students, largely from the South, voted seventy percent for Nixon.

The faculty, however, voted seventy percent for Kennedy. I voted for Nixon because I believed he showed strength against USSR leader Nikita Khrushchev in the "kitchen debate" in Moscow in 1959 by championing American capitalism. I was naïve. My political maturity had a way to go.

My years in college in the mountains of Tennessee in the early sixties could be wild and adventurous, of course. But Sewanee was also a time for growth and introspection. I did not have a formulated career path, but I lost myself in my major – English Literature – and history, philosophy, and political science. I liked the study of ideas, and my horizons broadened considerably. Later, after retiring from the Supreme Court, I would often say that I was a good lawyer and judge but that I had been one heck of an English major.

The Cuban missile crisis in 1962 rocked us all and was more than sobering. At supper one night at Sewanee, during the height of the crisis, "Waltzing Matilda" was piped into the student dining hall as a salute to the movie and book, *On the Beach,* which depicted Australia as the last surviving outpost following all out nuclear war.

There also was tension around civil rights. Racist Police Chief Bull Connor was hosing down Black students who were marching for their rights on the streets of Birmingham, Alabama. Plus, Freedom Riders were riding on buses throughout the South to demonstrate in favor of their rights and being attacked in places like Anniston, Alabama. And sit-ins to protest segregated restaurants began in Greensboro, North Carolina, and then were popping up everywhere. Racism in the South and its Jim Crow laws were under full attack, and my determination to fight the old system was front and center in my mind. But how?

During the summers, I generally did penance for my sins at school. One summer, I served as a lifeguard and general handyman at a small Episcopal Church camp in western Kansas. My peers at the camp were two Apache girls who did housekeeping and an eighteen-year-old from Dodge City who played organ for the chapel. Wheat fields, combines, tumbleweed, and wind were the backdrop for the experience. It was isolated and lonely. I loaded up on books I had not yet read: *All the*

King's Men, The Sound and the Fury, Farewell To Arms, and *Brave New World.* In that sense, it was a very successful summer.

My junior year, I excelled academically and won the silver cup for excellence in English Literature. That summer, my friend Howard Cockrill and I worked our way out west to the Seattle World's Fair. It was 1962, and our transportation was my mother's old Volkswagen Beetle. We would stop and visit friends for lodging and then wash dishes in Yellowstone Park Lodge or the Wind River Dude Ranch outside of Estes Park. After washing dishes at Wind River, I would be called upon to dance to "Put Your Little Foot" with the proprietress of the Ranch for the entertainment of the dudes. When I quit to move on, she blessed me out in no uncertain terms. "I could have gotten a wino to wash dishes," she said with an accusatory tone. The insult went right over my head. The 60s were upon us.

During my senior year in college, I received a quick course in integration. Sewanee's chaplain, the Rev. David Collins, took a few students, including myself, down to Atlanta to spend the weekend interacting with students at Morehouse College, the historically Black college. As it turned out, it was not that shocking or revolutionary an experience. Though kept apart from my Black peers by Jim Crow's laws for virtually all my life, we were all college students and had much in common. Conversations were easy, but some jabs were also taken. Southern gentlemen that we thought we were, we would stand up when Black women from Spelman College came into the room. I remember one Black male student remonstrating: "Sure, you stand up for our women now, but outside there, you beat us down." That comment was rare. Most of us – of both races – made an effort to have a realistic dialogue about the future of desegregation, though it was clear the Black students were activists and wanted changes made now. I often wondered whether Julian Bond or Samuel L. Jackson were among those who met with us since they both were at Morehouse in the early 1960s.

It was also during my senior year that I was selected to represent Arkansas as a nominee for a Rhodes Scholarship to study at Oxford University. There were two of us from Arkansas, and we gathered in

New Orleans with other pairs of nominees from other states in our district. Only four of the thirty-two would be selected. The first night in New Orleans, there was a cocktail party with members of the selection committee, and I sensed that I was not a top contender. The next day, however, I had a stellar interview with the committee, highlighted by my recitation of Cleopatra's praise for the slain Marc Antony in Shakespeare's *Antony and Cleopatra ("His Legs Bestrid the Ocean ...")*. I was back in the hunt, evidenced by the fact that the committee chair chose to sit next to me at the lunch that followed. Halfway through the dinner, I managed to carve my whole chicken into my lap. Neither of us said anything, but the silence after that said it all.

I did not get the Rhodes. But I was elected to Phi Beta Kappa and graduated magna cum laude from Sewanee. Next, I won a Woodrow Wilson Fellowship and chose to study English Literature at Columbia University in New York City. That proved to be a wonderful consolation prize for Oxford.

***

Over spring break my senior year, I decided I wanted to visit Charlie May Simon, who was best known for writing children's literature and whose home, known as Johnswood, was in central Arkansas. I had read her book, *Johnswood*, as well as *Life is My Song*, the autobiography of her deceased husband, Pulitzer Prize-winning poet John Gould Fletcher. Little did I know that fifteen years later Charlotte and I would buy Johnswood and live there for the next forty-three years.

Driving out to Johnswood, however, I decided an unannounced visit to Charlie May Simon was not a good idea. Instead, I turned around and paid an unannounced visit to John Gould Fletcher's sister, Adolphine Fletcher Terry.

Terry had always been an icon to me because of her work to form the Women's Emergency Committee in 1958-59. As she famously announced at the time: "The men have failed us. It's time to bring in the women." She lived in the historic Terry Mansion and greeted me at the front door. I explained I just wanted to talk about her family's work and my plans. We had a fine time over iced tea and that is when she told me, "Bob, try everything." To a twenty-one-year-old, that was music to my ears.

That same spring break, I double dated with a friend in Little Rock, T.L. Stebbins, who was at Harvard. T.L. had a date with Charlotte Banks, who was about to graduate from Briarcliff College in New York, and I had a date with one of Charlotte's friends.

I had met Charlotte over Christmas at a debutante party and had found her stylish and captivating with a personality that was engaging and entirely winsome. Later in the spring, I saw in the *Arkansas Gazette* that she had received the top honor at her graduation, Briarcliff's Trustees' Award for All-around Excellence. She was pictured, and I clipped that picture and carried it with me in my wallet. I declared to some at Sewanee that I was going to marry this woman.

I saw Charlotte once again at a wedding reception in early June and discovered that she too was going to New York. In her case, it was to study at Katherine Gibbs Secretarial School for Women, or Katie Gibbs, as it was more commonly known. I was elated. Not only would I have a woman whom I was smitten with in New York as a companion, but I had just found someone to type my master's thesis.

CHAPTER 5

Europe

But before Columbia, it was time to take the Grand Tour of Europe.

With a Sewanee friend, Charlie Tisdale, who was going to Oxford University to study English literature, I sailed on a Cunard Line ship to Southampton, England. On that voyage, Charles met a girl from Danville, Virginia, whom he promptly dubbed "Little Fox" and would later marry.

I have always had a biting, sarcastic tongue, and on the trip over I managed to taunt and infuriate two Princeton boys about the inferiority of their school. Suddenly, one of them grabbed and yanked a handful of my hair as I sat, mildly drunk, on a couch in the bar. A fighting move, no doubt. I got up, but it never came to blows. The offender was stumbling drunk. In my mind, I got the better of the exchange.

Prior to leaving on my trip, the redoubtable Fred Poe of Little Rock travel agent fame had sat at his desk, chain smoked Camels, and typed out fourteen pages of notes, front and back, about what I should see and do on my Grand Tour. He crafted the trip for me and was a genius in doing so. Not only did he know Europe well, but also had friends in most of the sites – the hotels, restaurants, and so forth. It was extraordinary. So, armed with Fred's notes and my Bible, that is, Frommer's *Europe On $5 A Day*, Charles and I attacked London.

Disembarking in Southampton, we took the train to London, where we explored the seamier side of the city but also the cultural "must sees." We also made a side trip to Stratford-upon-Avon and saw *Julius Caesar*. Then on to Oxford. As it happened, I had a cousin there on my mother's side and spent two nights with his family as Charles entered Oxford. I was gradually becoming accustomed to warm beer and pub food on my outings, discovering quickly that sandwiches and hamburgers were largely an American phenomenon.

I left Charles in Oxford and traveled solo to London where disaster struck. Riding the underground to my Grade C hotel, I hurriedly jumped off the train at my stop, only to discover I had left my travel satchel on the seat. That satchel had my passport, traveler's checks, Fred's notes, the Frommer book – you name it. The trip was technically at an end.

The next day I called the lost and found for the London Underground and got its address on Baker Street. Traveling to Sherlock Holmes's street, I entered the lost and found office and filled out a form. Moments later, the clerk handed me the lost satchel, which had my name and address on it. Everything was there. I said a prayer of thankfulness for British honesty and efficiency and set off to cross the English Channel by boat to Calais.

And so it happened. My formal college education crystallized into myriad shapes, sounds, voices, and expressions in Europe. I was very much at home there as I hitchhiked through the continent, knapsack on my back. The French and Italians were never very good at picking me up, even when I wore my herringbone sport coat and plaid tie. The Germans and Austrians were much better. When I reached a sticking point, that is, with no rides, I would simply hop a train. But my sleeping accommodations could vary. I never stayed in youth hostels, but I did sleep in a field outside of Orleans, an alley in Venice off a canal, a doorstep in Mainz, over an anthill in Lerici, Italy, where the poet Shelley drowned, and on a bahnhof bench in Munich. My sole weapon was a small switchblade knife I bought at a Little Rock pawn shop and never had to use but often had at the ready.

And I was always accompanied by a bottle of Vouvray, the French dessert wine I had taken a fancy to after my college years of drinking beer and bourbon. The Vouvray helped, as did the wide assortment of friends I made along the way. It was a frolic, and I learned if I were to survive, I would have to leave my introverted tendencies behind. On one occasion, I tried to pass myself off as British, but my cuffed trousers gave me away. Riding on the back of a Harley-Davidson motorcycle on the German autobahn was one harrowing experience. In a very real sense, the trip prepared me for what was to come in New York. I had successfully navigated England, France, Italy, Yugoslavia, Austria, and Germany.

When I eventually reconnected with Charles in Paris, we joined other Sewanee friends there. One friend in particular, Stuart McDaniel, who had a broad Atlanta accent, loudly complained that the French could not understand him, even when he spoke English. I had to confess that I couldn't understand him either.

The reunion in Paris was a blur. We celebrated in the extreme and threw glasses out of our second floor Left Bank hotel. We ended the evening in several cabarets in Pigalle. Somehow, I got separated from the group and got home by myself on the Paris Metro. Everyone else eventually materialized at the hotel. My switchblade knife was still in lock position. I term that night my one and only blackout.

The plan had been for me to end my tour in Spain, but I had been on my tour for two-and-a-half months, and it was time to go home. Having said that, I have still not been to Madrid or visited the Prado, the renowned museum. Maybe I was dead wrong to stop the trip when I did, but I certainly got back to the States in time for a historic event.

Flying to New York from Paris, my seatmates were a Black man and woman en route to Washington, D.C., for the August 28, 1963, March on Washington, where Martin Luther King would make his "I Have a Dream" speech. I admitted to them that I did not know much about the march since I had been overseas. They were surprised, but added this was a mammoth demonstration in support of civil rights. My immaturity kicked in, and I mentioned that some very good people like my grandfather happened to be racists. The couple should have turned their backs on me then and there, but they did not. They showed their class and said they understood and hoped that my grandfather would see the light and change his views. Then they turned their backs on me.

I grew up on my trip to Europe. For one thing, it was an amazing accomplishment for me to hitchhike alone through multiple countries and, at times, sleep on the street. (Of course, I had my switchblade knife with me.) A similar effort to hitchhike cross country in the States would have given me pause. Most people I met were helpful. Interestingly, my peers in Europe seemed more mature than their visiting American counterparts, who were prone to drink too much and act younger than they were. I was disappointed. Adjectives, though, don't begin to describe the treasures of Europe. And the opera and the theater. I even saw *My Fair Lady* in German.

CHAPTER 6

New York

Coming to New York after my education in Europe was a blessing. Unlike some hayseed character out of a William Styron novel venturing north, I was now unafraid to ask directions in my southern drawl or identify my home as Little Rock. That did not mean I was oblivious to how New Yorkers reacted to me or that the transition was entirely smooth. It was on-the-job training.

When I went to Columbia late one afternoon in September 1963 to register, I found there was no dormitory room awaiting me. There had always been a dormitory room for me at Sewanee, but Columbia was different. I must not have completed the required form for a room at John Jay Hall. A minor oversight. My only option was to walk down Broadway south from 116th Street and look for a hotel sign. When I saw the Harmony Hotel on 110th Street, my heart leapt up, and I got a room.

The hotel was basic and all I needed. After supper at a café off Broadway, I returned to finish a Thomas Hardy novel, *Jude the Obscure.* Fifteen minutes into the reading, shouts right out of *A Streetcar Named Desire* exploded down the hallway. I listened for a few minutes and then decided to do something about it. The couple, it was clearly a man and a woman and probably Black, were only a few doors away. Sliding off the bed and throwing on a bathrobe, I said to myself, "Whatever you do, don't say 'you all' when you confront them."

Their door was cracked, and I saw a man in his undershorts sitting on the bed and a woman in a slip standing in front of him, hands on her hips. "F-you, Jack," she said. "Black bitch," he threw back. Then they looked up at me.

"Will you all please be quiet?" I drawled. They did not answer but looked at me like I was from Mars. They were obviously dumbfounded.

I left their door open and walked to my room and heard nothing behind me. It later struck me that the Harmony Hotel might well be, at least in part, a place of "ill repute." No matter. There was no more noise, and I stayed for two more nights until I joined a new friend, David Leinsdorf, from Stanford who was renting an efficiency apartment on West 87th Street near West End Avenue and studying Mandarin Chinese at Columbia. We put a curtain between the two beds and somehow made it work. He lasted a semester.

The fall of 1963 was a combustible time in New York and much of the world. Civil rights protests and the responses were now more like pitched battles with a new brand of civil rights activists ratcheting up the rhetoric. In Vietnam, Buddhist monks were self-immolating on the streets of Saigon in protest to a corrupt Diem regime. And then came November 22 when President John F. Kennedy was shot and killed in Dallas. The world stopped as we mourned the loss of the vigorous and charismatic leader. We cried as the funeral cortege made its way down Pennsylvania Avenue with muffled drums keeping a somber beat. I told a graduate student friend, Nancy Flowers, that I liked the sound of muffled drums, and she added that to her long list of Bizarre Statements by Bob Brown.

History has shown us that in times of great political and social turmoil, the arts thrive. Think Homer's *Iliad* and the Trojan War. So it was in New York in the mid-sixties. There was popular music, of course, with the Beatles coming to New York for the first time, but theatre was also particularly vibrant on and off Broadway. Albert Finney in *Luther*, Alec Guinness in *Dylan*, Coleen Dewhurst in *Ballad of the Sad Cafe*,

James Earl Jones in *Baal*, Glenda Jackson in *Marat Sade*, Richard Burton in *Hamlet*, and on and on. The actors were all at the top of their game. Off Broadway, there were abundant treats like *The Trojan Women* directed by Michael Cacoyannis.

There was political upheaval as well. Lyndon Johnson was president now, and Bobby Kennedy had come to New York to run for a seat in the United States Senate. I was registered to vote in New York, and as much as I had been enamored of JFK, Bobby's political move to New York seemed too contrived and rendered him, in my mind, the ultimate carpetbagger. I voted for the Republican incumbent, Kenneth Keating, who lost decidedly in the 1964 race, but I redeemed myself some years later when I was positioned to help Bobby in his bid for the presidency.

***

The criteria for a master's degree in literature and comparative literature at Columbia University were fourfold: attendance at a certain number of classes plus a seminar in your area of concentration, which in my case was romantic literature; an approved master's thesis; passing a foreign language test; and passing a comprehensive written examination.

There were many memorable moments in my course work at Columbia. For instance, William York Tyndall, who was one of my favorite professors, would regale us with stories about Dylan Thomas's drunkenness (he retched a lot and stole clothes from his hosts) and the barbarians at the University of Texas who presumed to buy the manuscripts of James Joyce for their library. Tyndall exhibited New York arrogance at its worst, but I still liked him.

My master's thesis was entitled *The Sweetness of the Pain, a Study of the Female Symbol in the Poetry of John Keats*. It was a perfect preparation for life on the Arkansas Supreme Court, which I say with tongue planted firmly in cheek. I received honors, which meant I could continue for a PhD, which I later declined to do.

My Woodrow Wilson Scholarship, I thought, gave out after a year, and I still had not written my master's thesis or passed the comprehensive exam. Naïve as I was, I later found out I could have probably extended the scholarship for another year. My solution, though, was to get a job. There was only one ad in *The New York Times* for an English major, and it was for drafting amendments for group life insurance contracts for the Equitable Life Assurance Society in mid-town Manhattan. I applied and got the job.

After 87th Street, I had moved twice. First, to Paul Goodman's apartment on Broadway and 99th Street in January 1964. Goodman was a freelance anarchist, who was best known for his book, *Growing Up Absurd*, and was off to teach for a semester at the University of Wisconsin in Madison. He turned everything over to my two new roommates and me. His LP collection was incredible, ranging from Odetta to Schoenberg. I slept under an original Willem DeKooning. It was seventeen blocks to Columbia, which was a bit of a stretch for a walk, but doable.

Goodman's apartment was inspirational, as were the parties we had there. My two roommates and I lived in different worlds, which meant the guests at our parties were beyond eclectic. At one party, Fred Harrison, a friend visiting from Little Rock, recounted how one guest (who obviously was overserved) sat on a stool and barked at the wall.

Because Columbia did not demand much of its English graduate students on a daily basis, that first year, I drank in New York and went to lectures. My expertise soon became the French cinema. But that all ended with the new job and Paul Goodman's return. My next move was to Claremont Avenue north of Columbia by about seven blocks and closer to Barnard College, the Julliard School, and Union Theological Seminary. My subway stop was 125th Street and Broadway, which was essentially part of Harlem. My new roommate was Bob Stebbings, a Columbia Law student who was adventuresome and a good guy.

My social life in New York can best be described as varied and random. One close friend I dated, Ellie McNabb, lived on Tenth Street, just two doors down from playwright Edward Albee. The courtyard area behind Ellie's apartment looked like the set for the movie *Rear Window*. Perhaps that was a bad omen.

CHAPTER 7

Charlotte

Charlotte Anne Banks, whom I have already introduced, was from Fordyce in lower Arkansas, which is now known primarily for two things: a renowned crap shoot during the Second World War ("Four Dice on the Cotton Belt where the Rock Island Crosses") and as the hometown of Paul "Bear" Bryant, the legendary football coach at Alabama.

Charlotte grew up in a landmark four-story, Neoclassical mansion built in 1910 by her grandfather, A.B. Banks. Charles Thompson, the well-known Little Rock architect, designed the house, which was known as Pine Shadows (Photograph 5). Banks was one of Arkansas's most successful businessmen in both banking and insurance. At one time he was one of the wealthiest and most influential men in the South. He controlled fifty banks before losing his empire in the Great Depression of 1929. Banks re-established his insurance agency, The A. B Banks Company, and he prospered anew.

I reconnected with Charlotte shortly after my arrival in New York in 1963. The Harmony Hotel had been barely adequate housing for three days, and I urgently needed additional temporary lodging until I could move into a new apartment. I opted to call Charlotte, who was living with her Briarcliff college roommate, Anne Burroughs (Babcock) on East 72nd Street, and ask if I could sleep on their couch for a few days.

She said yes. At one point, Anne's father, Charles Burroughs, called from Norfolk, and I answered the telephone. This was the conversation:

Is Anne there?

No, she isn't.

Is Charlotte there?

No sir.

Well, by God, who the hell are you!?

I responded, but not convincingly.

Charlotte and I remained very good friends and, as such, saw each other occasionally. On a bitterly cold twenty-four-degree night, December 4, 1964, tragedy struck when Pine Shadows, her iconic home in Fordyce, caught fire in the basement and burned to the ground, a total loss. Her fifty-three-year-old father, Richard Banks, was killed, while her mother, Anne, managed to escape and save her paternal grandmother, Lottie Holmes Banks, who resided on the first floor.

Her roommate, Anne, called and gave me the horrific news. I did not see Charlotte until Christmas. Understandably she wanted to remain in Arkansas to help with the myriad of unsettling details following such a staggering loss and to be with her mother. It was minute to minute, day to day for them both. Through the caring generosity of lifelong friends such as Julia and Thomas Sparks, Joel and Judy Ledbetter, and her uncle and his wife, Catherine Anne and Walker Jones, they found themselves living in Fordyce, Little Rock, and Pine Bluff. Any plans in New York were the furthest thing from Charlotte's mind. But in mid-February her mother very selflessly and bravely sat her down and insisted that she must return to New York to resume her life (Photograph 6).

A renewed spark was ignited in me by the tragedy and Charlotte's return to the city. I now had an overwhelming desire to care for her. However, there was one major problem. Charlotte was seriously dating a New Yorker and was about to marry him. She already had an engagement picture taken by Arkansas native and close family friend, Tom Harding, who was a photographer at Bradford Bacharach.

Destiny, however, was on my side. Having picked Charlotte out in my Sewanee days, I became boldly determined and promptly mounted a full court press. I even used my father in one of his trips to New York to help win her over.

My quest took time but was at last successful, and she and her intended broke up. Just a few days after they went their separate ways, Charlotte and I were having dinner at Du Midi, an intimate and favorite restaurant on the Upper East Side. When I noticed an attractive woman in a full-length mink walk brusquely by, Charlotte suddenly went completely pale. It was the New Yorker's mother, whom she greatly admired and with whom she had a warm relationship.

There were other changes, as well. Slowly I felt a pull away from literature and a tug from the other side of my brain. Drafting contracts for the Equitable as opposed to studying Keats had something to do with it, but I also felt a desire to get more involved in a profession where I could have a tangible impact on society. Teaching at the college level surely had its attractions, but if the truth be known, I was tiring of literary analysis. One Saturday night in my apartment I decided on law school and the next week bought a book on the Law School Admissions Test (LSAT) at the bookstore near the West End Café on Broadway.

I like to tell the story that during the LSAT, when I was running out of time, I flipped to the back page and saw a pattern with my answers already given on the carbon page. I just continued that pattern for the next two or three questions I did not have time to answer. My ploy certainly did not hurt.

As it turned out, I scored in the nineties on the test under the old system of grading, and that, coupled with my imminent master's degree, made me a desirable commodity. I was accepted at the two schools where I had applied, the University of Virginia and Harvard, and I chose Virginia because it offered me a full scholarship. Harvard offered half the money I needed. And I was ready for the gentler life in the South. Moving to Virginia would prove to be a pivotal decision on my part and eventually led me back to Arkansas, as opposed to taking a shot at making it in New York. Had I not decided on law school, the Equitable Life Assurance Society had tested me for its management program and was primed to offer me a job.

In February of 1965, Malcolm X was assassinated in North Harlem. The former Nation of Islam lieutenant had split off from the Nation and its leader, Elijah Mohammed, and became their bitter enemy and rival. I had never given Malcolm X much thought. He struck me more as a fringe activist for Black Power, though his courtship of Mohammed Ali and Ali's conversion were certainly impressive.

What impressed me the night of his death were the Black luminaries who gathered in panel discussions on radio to pay tribute to this man – Ossie Davis, Ruby Dee, Harry Belafonte, and others. I was persuaded that Malcolm X had matured in his beliefs and was much more of a voice for African Americans than I had thought.

Before law school, I spent another summer in New York – the summer of 1965. Charlotte, soon to be my fiancée, was on a grand tour of her own in Europe with Anne. Still working at the Equitable, I wrote her every day. That summer an old college roommate from Sewanee, Gerry DeBlois, came to New York to work for the New York Civil Liberties Union. At the time, he was a law student at Tulane University. The NYCLU was simply a summer stint.

We spent more time in Greenwich Village than I had previously with a diverse group from his job, and he would wow me with stories like Alger Hiss's visit to the NYCLU to seek representation to void his perjury conviction related to communist activity. He was turned down flat.

CHAPTER 8

Charlottesville

When Charlotte returned in August, we spent time in Virginia Beach with her mother and aunt, Rachael Jones Williams. It was there I proposed to her, and she answered in two words: "You bet." From there, I sallied forth to Charlottesville, while she returned to New York to work at McKenzie and Company. Of course, Charlotte already had the Bacharach engagement picture she could use (Photograph 7). We would marry the following year on June 18, 1966.

Charlottesville was a complete cultural shock for me. From roaming the streets and bars of New York and living in bohemian venues, I was now back in a dorm room with a roommate, Bill Quillian. His father, also Bill Quillian, was president of Randolph-Macon Woman's College (now Randolph College) in Lynchburg, Virginia. In classes at the University of Virginia, a coat and tie were required. The first-year class size was over one hundred, and we had two women and one Black enrolled. That would swiftly change during the next decade. For now, it was a throwback. From Keats, I turned to courses in contracts, torts, property, criminal law, civil procedure. Nothing could have been more foreign to me. And I struggled.

During my first year at law school, Charlotte and I would visit back and forth between New York and Charlottesville, and in Little Rock, of course, over the holidays. It was a long-distance relationship, but in the spring of 1966 planning for our June 18 wedding began in earnest. Old friends would serve as groomsmen and bridesmaids, although my best friend, Thurston Roach, was serving in Vietnam and could not be there.

We got married in Trinity Episcopal Church in Pine Bluff, the church home of Charlotte's mother's family for generations. My father performed the ceremony, and her much-loved uncle, Pine Bluff native Walker Jones, walked her down the aisle. Interestingly, my father, who was very "low church," instructed the full choir that the anthem would not be sung in Latin, but only in English. Accordingly, "Sanctus, Sanctus, Sanctus" from Gounod's Faust became "Holy, Holy, Holy."

That night after we left the wedding reception to drive to Dallas for our flight to Mexico for our honeymoon, the wedding party and guests celebrated in fine and true Southern fashion. Our friend, Rusty Wilson, was injured in a freak electrical accident after he left the reception with his date, Elsa Crocker. His car was not put in park and ran into a tree. This caused an electrical wire to break free and fall on my friend's head and hand. The quick presence of mind of a neighbor, Floyd Fulkerson, in lifting my friend off the wire with a rubber hose saved his life. Tragically, Rusty's hands were badly maimed.

Mexico City and the beaches of Acapulco provided our honeymoon venue. I suffered an extremely severe sunburn after unwittingly taking the advice of a fellow beach dweller to lather myself in coconut oil. I fried. I could not wear shoes. People turned away and winced. The deleterious impact of the sunburn on my honeymoon was obvious. We limped back to Dallas where we were forced to unexpectedly recuperate for three nights with Charlotte's welcoming cousins, Jac and Sue Austin.

Returning to Charlottesville for my second year of law school, and without Charlotte seeing it beforehand, we moved into a second-story rented flat off Ivy Road. It had a full view from our kitchen window of the Hawkins Funeral Home's back entrance, which was used for the hearse and the delivery of the deceased. Yet, we were quite happy there, despite the funeral home view, the ever-present mice, and our landlady on the first floor with her demented housekeeper, Sootie.

Charlotte got a job as administrative assistant to the head mistress at St. Anne's School, now St. Anne's- Belfield School, her secondary school alma mater. She was next hired by the UVA Department of Pediatrics, where she was mentored by its highly regarded Vanderbilt-trained chairman, Dr. Robert Merrill, and thrived. He quickly recognized her inherent potential as something more than a secretary, for which she had been trained. I continued to work hard at law school. It was all getting easier.

After my third year in law school had begun, we stayed in Arkansas for an extra week because my father had invited the Archbishop of Canterbury, Michael Ramsay, and his wife, Joan, to visit Little Rock. No doubt the history of Little Rock and race was a major draw for the archbishop.

The Ramsays came for about three days and stayed in our house. My parents had a dinner party with the Ramsays, Governor Rockefeller, and his wife, Jeannette. It was all beyond exciting.

The watershed time for Little Rock was capped by an ecumenical service at Robinson Auditorium. The service was a complete success, in part because it was important to have all denominations and races participate. It reenforced my belief that we all could be one under God. At one point before the service, I mentioned to *Arkansas Gazette* columnist Richard Allin that the press coverage had been exemplary. His answer was: "My gosh, Bob, he's the Archbishop of Canterbury."

One humorous event during the visit involved Charlotte and our housekeeper, Ruby. As Charlotte was coming down the back stairs at the Bishopstead, Ruby held up large purple boxer shorts, chuckled, and exclaimed, "Look! It's the Archbishop's drawers!"

The other event during my third year in law school that made an impression on me was an Honor Council trial I prosecuted. The University of Virginia at the time had zero tolerance for lying, cheating, or stealing by a student. The student involved was challenged for cheating on a French test.

My case was simple. The accused student's answers were "strikingly similar" to those of a student two rows ahead of him, including the wrong answers. I argued my case to the Student Honor Council, and the accused was found not culpable. Two weeks later I got a call from the chair of the Honor Council, Henry Massie, who was an old friend from St. Christopher's. He said the student had just been accused of making a bomb scare to avoid taking a test in the targeted building. He was suspended or expelled, Massie said, and I heard nothing more about it. I can only speculate on how that student turned out.

I like to say the sixties missed the University of Virginia, but that is not altogether true. They just hit the campus late – 1967 and 1968 to be exact. Vietnam loomed large but the assassination of Martin Luther King traumatized all of us. Charlotte and I marched before a funeral service for King at Chapel Hill, North Carolina, (we were visiting Sewanee friends) and watched as fires broke out in the nation's capital and across the country. I also heard a particularly riveting talk by NAACP Chair Roy Wilkins at the Law School about the King legacy and what we, as lawyers, could do in the courts to further the civil rights cause.

In retrospect, Virginia was a wonderful experience. There was the law school education, of course, which was exemplary, but also a surrounding culture that was enticing. There were social club activities and touch football games. There were forays to steeplechases as well as polo competitions and rugby matches. That was all an education in itself.

We left Charlottesville in June of 1968. I had decided to work in Little Rock for a law firm I had clerked for the previous two summers, Chowning, Mitchell, Hamilton & Burrow. Atlanta had been the other appealing venue, but we chose Little Rock. I was also going to support Bobby Kennedy for president. It was on the trip home to Little Rock that we awoke in a motel at Sewanee, turned on television, and saw Frank Mankiewicz standing on the trunk of his car reporting that RFK had been shot and was in critical condition. He later died.

Again, the world shook beneath our feet, and we were devastated. There was now no viable Democratic opponent to take on Richard Nixon. LBJ had taken himself out of the race. Gene McCarthy's sole issue was Vietnam. Hubert Humphrey seemed too entwined with Johnson.

Charlotte and I arrived in Little Rock heavy hearted and stayed in my parents' guesthouse, where I began a six-week stint studying for the Arkansas Bar Exam. I took the exam in July and made the almost fatal mistake of celebrating much too exuberantly the Saturday night after I finished studying. But the three-day exam actually began on Monday, so I was hungover all day Sunday. Then, somewhat wobbly, I took the test and passed.

CHAPTER 9

Europe Redux

There was one more trip left in us before I settled in to practice law. Europe beckoned again, and this time it was to be Great Britain, with two weeks in England, two in Scotland, and two in Ireland.

My father was again attending the Lambeth Conference for Episcopalian and Anglican bishops in London that meets every ten years, and he and my mother were staying in the Goring Hotel. They were able to reserve a room for us there for a few nights at the beginning of the trip.

Two events stand out in my mind during our short stay. The first was a grand dinner party that my parents and Bishop Christoph Keller, Jr., Bishop Coadjutor of Arkansas, and his wife, Polly, had at the Goring for several close episcopate friends who were attending the conference. A dinner party with several English bishops and their wives, replete with their very British manners and expressions was completely entertaining. ("Have a care, Bishop Brown.")

The second memorable event was our trip by train to Canterbury one Sunday afternoon for evensong at the majestic Canterbury Cathedral. Then-Presiding Bishop of the Episcopal Church, our dear old friend John Hines, gave the sermon, and the Archbishop of Canterbury, Michael Ramsey, officiated. The choir sang the spiritual "Were You There?", no doubt in honor of the presiding bishop.

After the service, we had tea with the Hineses and the Ramsays and then traced the steps with the dean of the cathedral where Thomas à Beckett fled Henry II's knights before he was murdered. Unlike Beckett lore, Beckett did not die stoically, but, according to the dean, he ran for his life. When he fell, "The stones turned black with lice and blood."

Back in London for dinner I was in a quandary about how to go forward. Charlotte's sage advice was simple: "Let's go." We had already rented an Austin Mini. We drove out of the city at midnight for my first time on the left side of the road, a truly sobering experience. The round-abouts were especially daunting. We managed it, though, throughout England. We drove west and then north into Scotland, staying most nights in bed and breakfasts. It was a delightful way to experience the two countries and fraternize with our hosts over yeoman breakfasts.

The one exception to the B&B's was Hartlebury Castle, which housed friends of my parents, the Bishop of Wooster, Charles Edwards, and his wife, Louise. The castle had a moat but also much of literary great Alexander Pope's personal library, which I eagerly scanned. It was all beyond surreal, and myriad ghosts marched through the house and into my dreams at night.

My intense study of English literature for seven years again paid huge dividends. There was Jane Austen in Winchester Cathedral, Shake-speare in Stratford-upon-Avon, Sir Walter Scott in Abbottsford, and a whole array of literal references in Westminster Abbey and Oxford University.

In Scotland, we saw the Tattoo at Edinburg Castle, the heather in bloom as we ventured north to Inverness, and then the construction of Cunard's masterpiece, the Queen Elizabeth II, in the Glasgow ship-yards. We had crossed the Atlantic on the last voyage of the Queen Elizabeth; hence, there was a certain continuity in seeing her successor still in dry dock and almost seaworthy.

While in Edinburgh in September, Charlotte and I were asked to sign a petition opposing the Vietnam War, which we did. But we were also repeatedly asked about the Democratic Convention in Chicago and the tumult between the Chicago police and Mayor Richard Dailey on one side and the anti-war protesters on the other. "What is happening to your country?" was the anguished inquiry. We had no real answer. Nor do we today in 2022 with racial division, the coronavirus pandemic, and the assault on the nation's capital, when the same question is asked.

Next, we traveled to the Isle of Skye, where I imagined a latter-day Heathcliff off in the fog roaming the surrounding moors. Dublin followed after a brief flight, and James Joyce, Oscar Wilde, and Yeats all hovered over and around us. After numerous renditions of "Danny Boy," we drove south to the Ring of Kerry and then up the west coast to Yeats Country (Sligo) and to Ashford Castle and Shannon Airport for our flight back to the United States.

CHAPTER 10

Back Home

In October 1968, I settled in with my new law firm in Little Rock and began the tedious practice of getting summonses and subpoenas issued by the sheriff and court clerk; filing lawsuits; having judgments, orders and decrees signed by a judge; and doing spot legal research for the partners. Charlotte and Tina Poe, wife of Fred Poe, had become close friends, and it was not long before she went to work at their well-respected agency, Poe Travel, as a travel agent and Fred's assistant. It was a perfect fit for someone who loved people, travel, and had attention to detail.

It was now time for my second foray into Arkansas politics. Our governor was still Winthrop Rockefeller, scion of the legendary New York Rockefellers and the man who would launch Arkansas into the New South. He was another excellent reason for me to return to Arkansas. Rockefeller's legislative program was beyond ambitious: a nine percent rate for the state income tax; reorganization of state agencies into more efficient departments; free textbooks and kindergarten for public schools; a state human resources department to better relations between the races; more money for the state's medical center; and a local option liquor-by-the-drink law. The liquor-by-the-drink law passed, but the rest of his programs ran into an old guard, democratic party buzz saw in the General Assembly.

Rockefeller, after all, was attempting to countermand much of what his predecessor, Orval Faubus, had done. Faubus's segregationist policies had besmirched the state, and Rockefeller was doing his best to erase the stains. Three days following the assassination of Martin Luther King in April 1968, Rockefeller participated in a Sunday memorial service with Black pastors and other religious leaders like my father on the State Capitol steps to eulogize and praise King. He was the only governor in America to do so. He urged reconciliation and adherence to what King had preached. It was an especially gallant and courageous thing for him to do.

I was beyond impressed with Rockefeller. Though his legislative program had faltered, his commitment to racial equality had not. He appointed African Americans to his personal staff: Walter Cunningham, Henry Jones (later a United States Magistrate), Perlesta Hollingsworth, and Ozell Sutton, who had called my father from Memphis after the King assassination. Sonny Walter was appointed director of the Office of Economic Opportunity and Rev. Emery Washington became director of the Education Department. The state had turned an important corner.

Rockefeller had an opponent in November 1968, Democrat Marion Crank, who had solid old guard credentials, and the governor, as already noted, had political liabilities. He was a carpetbagger from New York, a Republican, one of the world's wealthiest men, a liberal on race, divorced, drank to excess, and had done a eulogy extolling Martin Luther King.

My political guru in those days was the Democrat activist, Brownie Ledbetter. She called me in early October and convinced me to "go door to door in my precinct and campaign for Win." I was more than willing, and Rockefeller won by a very slim majority. Two years later, Brownie called me back and said I had to do the same thing for a little-known Charleston lawyer, Dale Bumpers, who was running against Rockefeller.

Her reasoning was simple. Where Rockefeller's vision for Arkansas had been inspired, implementing that vision through an old guard

Democrat legislature had been well-nigh impossible. She thought that a gallant, young Lochinvar, riding in from the west, like Bumpers, would be more successful, and that proved to be exactly what happened. Again, I obliged her. Bumpers was elected, took Rockefeller's proposed programs as his legislative agenda, and got most of them passed. Later, my friendship with Brownie would be tested when I ran against Judge Judith Rogers for the Arkansas Supreme Court.

Working for the Chowning Law Firm gave me a good taste of a general law practice, and I worked closely with Dubb Hamilton and Will Mitchell, who were senior partners. But my juices flowed in a different direction. Over the next two years, I participated in liberal causes like legal aid – then in its infancy – and flirted with joining an integrated law firm, Rotenberry and Walker.

There was also the controversial production of *Hair* being brought to Robinson Auditorium in Little Rock with its nudity, drug culture, four letter words, and anti-war sentiments. Under city ordinances, a three-person ethics committee could block the performance by labeling it obscene, and the committee did exactly that.

Phil Kaplan, a legitimate legal bomb thrower at the time, sued the city of Little Rock on the basis that blocking *Hair* on obscenity grounds violated free speech, particularly since obscenity was not well defined under the city ordinance. I committed to sign the complaint with several other lawyers. But I had to tell my conservative law firm what I planned.

To his credit, Dubb Hamilton went to another senior partner, Frank Chowning, and explained what I was about to do. He described *Hair* as a play where at one point a woman bared her breasts, and he demonstrated what he meant by opening his jacket and flapping it. Chowning laughed, and that was my answer.

But before *Hair* descended on Little Rock, I had made a decision to leave the Chowning Firm and join the prosecuting attorney's office as a special deputy prosecutor. Jim Guy Tucker, the newly elected prosecuting attorney, was twenty-seven and I was twenty-nine. I was excited about the idea of joining someone near my age with a young team and progressive agenda.

Charlotte initially was incredulous about my decision, as were most of my friends, but she quickly embraced the idea.

The way Tucker explained it, I would be one of several new deputy prosecutors who would form a special circuit court division. We would clear out the old Pulaski County jail by trying the cases of those incarcerated. Many of those jailed were booked under the dubious category of "S" which stood for "Suspicion." That was clearly not a bona fide basis for arrest and incarceration. Circuit judges would be pulled in from around the state to try the cases. Money was provided for the extra prosecutors and judges under the 1968 Federal Omnibus Crime Act.

The move landed me on a different planet. My fellow deputies and I were all young, really too young for the job. Most of us had long hair and sideburns and wore bell-bottomed trousers before they became fashionable at the courthouse. Rather than rockabilly, our music of choice was Credence Clearwater Revival, the Stones, and The Doors. We did not hesitate to speak our minds. All of this bred a mutual distrust between us and the police officers and courthouse personnel we worked with. We were considered hippies who smoked pot and identified more with the criminals than the police. At the same time, we brought a breath of fresh air to the dank county offices and criminal justice system.

Occasionally, Tucker and other deputies would go on police raids and kick down the doors of their prey. Dangerous stuff. One deputy, Clarence Cash, joined a raid of the state fair concession stands for illegal gambling and confiscated an array of stuffed animals, which he jammed into his office the following Monday morning. John Butt, a deputy and Vietnam veteran, would offer visitors beer or apple pie stored in his desk drawer, where he also kept his pistol. (John later died tragically by falling off a cliff in the Ozark Mountains.)

Illegal gambling was not limited to the state fair. In North Little Rock, The Diamond Club (aka The 609 Club) operated as a full-blown casino under the watchful eye of Mayor Casey Laman. Tucker, as district prosecuting attorney, and Sonny Dillahunty, as United States

Attorney, were jockeying to close the club and bring Laman down. The club closed, but Laman was never charged.

Prostitution was a different matter. Tucker investigated a North Little Rock police captain for "running girls." As part of that investigation, Tucker and I interrogated two madams, and took custody of their "Trick Books." The names in those books included some well-known Little Rock businessmen and leaders. Tucker and I decided that I would be the one to take the books home and hide them, because they would not be safe in our offices. I hid them under my bed at home, and Charlotte and I slept over that trove, with one eye open, for several months.

Dramatic events would occur as part of that investigation. Once, when I was interrogating an alleged prostitute who was fifteen and pregnant, the girl's water broke in my office, and we quickly hailed a cab to take her to the closest hospital.

When I prosecuted for that year and a half, police corruption plagued the city. The most celebrated case I tried was the Sandbar Rape Case where three Black teenagers were charged with beating and raping two white girls on a sandbar on the south side of the Arkansas River. The three teenagers were arrested and confessed after police questioning. An issue quickly arose of whether the confessions had been unlawfully beaten out of them by police detectives in violation of the United States Supreme Court's *Miranda* decision, which prohibited coerced confessions. Racial prejudice lay at the heart of the case and divided the city and the state for that matter, mostly along racial lines.

The case was tried by a Pulaski County jury three times, and mistrials were declared each time. In the first trial, the death penalty was requested by Tucker's predecessor as prosecutor, Richard Adkisson, who would later be a circuit judge and then Chief Justice of the Arkansas Supreme Court. That trial ended in a hung jury, almost evenly divided. Eminent civil rights attorney and icon Wiley Branton, who originally hailed from Pine Bluff and now worked in Washington, D.C., accompanied by Little Rock attorney and NAACP Legal Defense Fund attorney John Walker, represented the defendants. Branton's first closing argument to the jury focused on the death penalty and graphically described death by electrocution. "Why is it that police officers in particular like to watch electrocutions?" he argued.

The second mistrial was caused by deputy prosecutor David Hale, who asked the jury panel during jury selection whether they would be influenced by the demonstration in favor of the defendants that attorney Walker had organized on the courthouse grounds. Several hundred people had appeared that morning to protest the innocence of the three defendants. The circuit judge ruled that Hale's question was unduly prejudicial and declared a mistrial.

By the time of the third trial, Tucker had been elected prosecuting attorney. I prosecuted the case as his deputy. In this trial the death penalty was not an issue for rape. In my prosecution, two trials in effect took place. The first dealt with whether the defendants had committed the crime. The second was whether the police detectives had beaten the defendants to elicit the damning confessions.

Jury selection, with questions by counsel known as *voir dire*, was of prime importance because of the racial overtones that roiled the case. As part of *voir dire*, answers to questions from attorneys by prospective jurors could be unintentionally revealing. When I asked a prospect whether he could vote for a life sentence for the crime of rape, the answer he gave was, "Just for rape?" I dismissed that prospect. Another time, Branton asked a prospect about his views on justice regarding rape. The answer was the Good Book says rape is a sin and perpetrators should be punished. Branton leaned over to me and whispered, "Lord, save us from the Christians."

It was an article of faith that a Black juror would most likely vote to acquit, and so questioning of prospective Black jurors was very intense by both sides. Toward the end of the selection process, I was low on automatic challenges, and a youngish Black business operator appeared balanced in his answers and objective. I accepted him as a juror. Walker immediately rushed out of the office, obviously to check on the man. When he came back, he smiled at Branton. That was not good news to me.

The case took almost two weeks to try. At the end, the jury hung up once more by a vote of 10 to 2. I was told one of the two hold-outs for conviction was the Black juror whom I had accepted. About a year later, Jim Guy Tucker declined to prosecute the charges against the three defendants again and agreed to release them based on time served in the county jail.

The question I revisit on occasion is whether justice was served. It was a brutal crime against the two girls by a gang of teenagers. The three arrested spent more than two years in jail. They confessed, but there was evidence that the confessions were involuntary and that they had been beaten by police detectives in clear violation of the *Miranda* decision. It was known in the prosecutor's office in 1970-71 that certain detectives in Gale Weeks's police department beat suspects. I think it was Winston Churchill who said a criminal justice system based on confessions is no justice system at all. And so it was. Perhaps justice was served. But probably not.

In December 1971 and January 1972, Charlotte and I, with the blessing of Poe Travel, took a break for four weeks and traveled to Switzerland, Austria for Christmas, then to Hungary, and finally to what was then Czechoslovakia. Our first stop was Zurich, where we discovered that my bag had traveled with the luggage of several students going to Tel Aviv. My trip was immediately in jeopardy. We had a friend in Zurich because of Charlotte's travel connections who flew for Swiss Air. His nickname was Tex, and he advised Delta in no uncertain terms that I was his friend and recovery of my bag was of the utmost importance. The bag was returned within twenty-four hours. It had been thoroughly searched. An unclaimed bag in Tel Aviv most definitely set off signals.

The train ride through the snow-crested Alps to Salzburg was magical. We arrived and checked into our hotel, Goldener Hirsch (translated the Golden Stag), on the narrowest of streets and basked in the moment. Mozart and Schubert were in the air. We lived on champagne, strudel, and Sacher tortes.

Then on to Vienna for Richard Strauss's *Die Fledermaus* on New Year's Eve at the Opera House, followed by New Year's Day at the Musikverein and a performance by the Vienna Symphony Orchestra of Strauss and more Strauss. Budapest and Prague came next. Budapest had the better food, but Prague, which was about to break out of its Soviet chains, had Pilsner beer, and was vibrant and alive.

We heard Wagner in Budapest and smuggled compelling private art out of Prague artists' studios through our Czech connections (we had not bought it from the state or paid the required state tax). Most of that art still hangs in our living room at Johnswood. I put the contraband in Charlotte's bag, which was not searched on the conveyor belt by the police. Mine was. Shortly after that, we read about two boys going to a Soviet prison for attempting to smuggle a souvenir bear out of the USSR.

We made it to London and, in addition to partaking of West End theater, we were destined to see Stanley Kubrick's futuristic film *A Clockwork Orange*. On our previous visit there, we had sat mesmerized watching *2001: A Space Odyssey*.

When I returned, I helped manage Tucker's campaign for state attorney general with Clarence Cash. It was my first real immersion in a statewide campaign. Tucker had received abundant media attention as prosecuting attorney and was well known, at least in central Arkansas, which was a decided plus. At the same time, he was considered liberal and pro-union. His opponent was Bill Thompson from Fort Smith, also a prosecutor, who had strong political connections. It promised to be a donnybrook, which it was. It gave me a road map on how to win a statewide election.

"It's television, Stupid," I came to understand, to borrow from the James Carville comment about the economy in Clinton's race for the presidency in 1992. Letters, endorsements, newspaper ads, even radio were way down the list for voter impact. Both Tucker and Thompson were naturals on television, but Thompson had a calm, cool demeanor whereas Tucker had Robert Redford looks and exuded excitement. Tucker won by seven thousand votes. It was said after the race that if

Thompson had borrowed money in the final days and poured it into television ads he might well have taken the prize. But he did not. He was not a gambler, and Tucker had gone all out.

After that victory in May 1972, I knew I had no interest in going to the attorney general's office with Tucker. Nor did the law practice thrill me. I had tasted the sweet fruit of politics, and I was hooked. It was, after all, a young person's game, and I was thirty-one.

CHAPTER 11

The Gentleman from Charleston

Dale Bumpers, from Charleston, Arkansas, had rocketed to the governor's office in 1971, and with his youthful charm and Rockefeller's program he was poised to refurbish Arkansas's image. He was already known as "the Giant Killer" having slain Orval Faubus and Win Rockefeller. I was young enough and heard the siren call beckoning me to join the governor's staff. Tom McRae, who had already made his mark in the Peace Corps in Nepal and as director of Model Cities in Texarkana, was Bumpers's chief of staff. I knew him slightly and made the call to him offering my services. Meetings were held, and I was welcomed aboard.

Right off the bat, I was dubbed the "Legal Aide for Bumpers." Among my jobs was to be the liaison with the prisons and particularly with Superintendent Terrell Don Hutto. The prisons were always time bombs threatening to detonate at any moment over any issue. Winthrop Rockefeller had instituted major reforms such as bringing in free world personnel to run the prisons as opposed to trusties who were prisoners themselves. Hutto was a hardliner as superintendent who ruled with an iron hand. And there were no riots during his tenure (Photograph 8).

Bumpers and I would travel to the prisons on occasion to show the flag. Hutto would always remind Bumpers to also talk to the guards and thank them for their work. Bumpers clearly preferred conversations with the prisoners. That's where his sympathies lay.

I also handled pardons, commutations of sentences for parole eligibility, and extradition matters for Bumpers. These issues, especially the pardons and commutations, were sensitive matters, and Bumpers was very thorough in his decision making. At the same time, he had interesting theories about who should be eligible. On one occasion, he remarked that an applicant who was convicted of rape might be a good candidate for release since he was approaching the age of forty which meant he was losing his sex drive. Bumpers's observation caused us all to roll our eyes.

Joining the Bumpers parade was exhilarating. Nobody was a better speaker on the hustings. Not Jimmy Carter. Not Bill Clinton. No one. He could preach, but more importantly, he could entertain. In his jokes, no one was safe. Country hicks, the elderly, women, Asians, ministers, the unsophisticated, or unintelligent. Bumpers would get right up to the line in his joke telling. Sometimes, he would cross it. He was never politically correct, and that was part of his appeal. Today, in some venues full of wokeness, he would be hooted off the stage.

In private, he was equally as funny, if more bawdy. Unimpressive men were "numb nuts." All women were "doll." If he had a nerve-wracking experience, he might say "You couldn't get an oily spike up my _ _ _." Or a particularly convincing salesman might be described as "He could sell a whore a bean sandwich," whatever that meant. He was wonderfully descriptive.

And he recognized and used talent: Men like Richard Arnold, his legislative coordinator, before spending nearly thirty years as a federal judge, and Tom (his chief of staff), but also his young nephew by marriage, Archie Schaffer.

What quickly became obvious was that there were two rival camps in the governor's office. The first was the political camp casually overseen by Archie. The second was the policy camp supervised by Tom and his team. I floated somewhere in the middle. Archie worked with the legislature and on Bumpers's political future. Tom, for the most part, did not like or trust the members of the General Assembly and had little rapport with them. That was an obvious disadvantage for the governor's chief of staff. A relationship with the legislative leadership was essential. Archie had it. Tom did not.

Where Tom was effective was in his organizational ability. Within the governor's office, he had staff members who acted as liaisons for the department heads. At times, though, it became confusing who was setting the policy: the department head or the Governor's staff member. And conflicts did arise, which I suspect mirrors what happens in many executive staffs.

Bumpers's political skills, however, were daunting. Using a political guru from Memphis, Deloss Walker, the two men cobbled together a strategy to never mount a negative campaign or attack an opponent. Rather, Bumpers would do a five-minute, issue-oriented colloquy for the radio with Deloss, or talk directly to the camera and tell people what he would do for them. Using colloquialisms ("You need somebody you can tie to") and homespun stories taken right off the porch of his father's general store in Charleston, he was captivating on radio and television.

The media emphasized his best attributes. The television camera flattered him with his facial bone structure that had a hint of his part Cherokee heritage. Intelligent, youthful, and articulate with southern charm in spades, he was a political force to be reckoned with.

* * *

Sarge Shriver or Tom Eagleton? Today they are a blip on the political screen, but in 1972 they were headline news. Eagleton, a United States Senator from Missouri, had been selected by Democrat presidential nominee George McGovern to be his running mate, but then reports of the senator's bouts with depression and mental health treatments like electric shock therapy surfaced, and Eagleton pulled himself out of the race. A mini convention had to be held to accept McGovern's second vice president selection, and quickly.

In July 1972, the convention was held in Miami Beach, Florida, and I accompanied Dale as his aide. It was all that a convention should be but handled extremely poorly. Gary Hart and Jeanne Westwood were there as McGovern's campaign managers, Jessie Jackson was there in his dashiki, and Larry O'Brien was convention chair.

McGovern settled on Shriver as his new running mate. Shriver, a Yale-educated diplomat who married into the Kennedy family, was a lead architect in the War on Poverty in the 1960s, helping to launch the Peace Corps and programs like the Jobs Corp, Head Start, and Upward Bound. But McGovern made his selection speech at three in the morning. Not exactly prime time. And the Kennedy connection wasn't enough. Nixon and Agnew went on to swamp the Democratic ticket in November. Yet it became clear at this mini convention that Dale was a rising star in the party, and he was treated as such. Multiple delegates formed an eddy around him wherever he went. It was exciting and exhilarating.

* * *

It was the early seventies, and Charlotte threw herself into work at Poe Travel, the Junior League, the Episcopal church, and the interesting friends we had developed in our new jobs and volunteer work.

As a legislative aide, I helped coordinate the legislative package for Bumpers for the 1973 session. Bumpers used warhorses like former Little Rock Mayor Martin Borchert and Senator Ben Allen, who knew where all the bodies were buried. He had also used Brad Jesson and Doug Smith from Fort Smith in 1971, and in 1973 he relied on Joe Woodward from Magnolia and Tommy Sparks of Fordyce fame. They were all his point guards and lobbied the legislators on his behalf. Bumpers, like Tom McRae, had little respect for the old guard rank-and-file legislators, but he kept his comments in check other than to say to confidants, "They would steal the dome off the capital if it weren't attached."

Meeting with legislators one on one, which Archie lined up and ushered in, was Bumpers's strong suit. Richard and I assisted in putting together his legislative package consisting of administration bills that were considered first by the General Assembly. Free textbooks and kindergarten as well as a $30 million appropriation for the University of Arkansas for Medical Sciences (UAMS) cemented Bumpers's legacy as the education and health care governor. State coffers were full, and Bumpers took advantage of it. He had already passed the increase in the state income tax and reorganization of state government within sixteen departments in the 1971 session.

In 1973, after the legislative session, Bumpers traveled the state with his aide, Jim Lamonica. That year, I was his principal speechwriter. I would craft magnificent speeches with quotations from Thomas Jefferson, Scotty Reston, and Walt Whitman only to find out from Jim that Bumpers used the first paragraph containing facts about Arkadelphia, Clarendon, Mountain Home, or wherever he was going and then ad-libbed the rest based on standard remarks he had already calibrated. But that rejection was not as bad as what happened to Tom McRae on one trip. According to Jim, he and Tom were with Bumpers as a State Police security officer drove them to a speaking venue. Bumpers began reading the speech and after two or three paragraphs he crushed it in his hands and cried out, "Who wrote this crap?" Shyly, Tom murmured, "I did." At that, Bumpers leaned over, picked up the pages, and began smoothing out the sheets. He then read the rest of the remarks (Photograph 9).

After passing the Rockefeller program in the general legislative sessions in 1971 and 1973 and holding off attacks on the state treasury by old guard legislators, the core issue in 1974 was Bumpers's political future. Would he run for another two-year term as governor in 1974 or run for the United States Senate against J. William Fulbright, the incumbent and foreign policy icon who had opposed the Vietnam War?

His dilemma was cause for heated speculation, and no one seemed to really know what his decision would be. Two days before he was to decide, I asked his wife, Betty, what he was going to do. We were in my car in the governor's mansion parking lot, and I sensed she did not know. But she looked at me earnestly and said, "It really doesn't make any difference, Bob. Either way, he'll be unhappy." It was an interesting insight into the brooding Arkansas wunderkind.

When Bumpers finally announced he was running for the United States Senate, some Arkansas liberals dubbed it fratricide. Longtime friend and supporter, Tommy Sparks, told him that as a matter of conscience he would have to support Fulbright. Bumpers said he understood but had little to do with him after that.

My charge during the ensuing campaign was to organize the Second Congressional District, which was Little Rock and Central Arkansas, where Bumpers was insanely popular. Our organization in Pulaski County included precinct captains and transportation to the polls for predominantly Black neighborhoods.

At one point, Betty Bumpers received word from Democratic friends in Searcy, which was part of my district, that nothing was being done on Bumpers's behalf in White County. Betty called me and we "saddled up" to ride to Searcy to assess the campaign. It appeared to me that the older Democratic Party leaders wanted to wrest control from the younger county coordinators like Judge Jim Hannah (later Supreme Court Chief Justice) and Leroy Froman. Putting out brush fires and smoothing ruffled egos was part of my role. . . and Betty's. My assessment, after the visit, was that all was well in White County.

There was also a network of political bosses, especially in Black precincts, who expected to be paid "walking around money." This was the get-out-the-vote effort, where the bosses were deemed necessary. But you had to thread the needle of paying for legitimate transportation costs like gas and drivers to take voters to the polls versus simply paying the ward boss a large sum for his or her "support." We threaded that needle adroitly but were ever mindful of the fact that often we really did not know how the money was being used.

The campaign itself sparked considerable controversy. Bumpers and Fulbright were very aligned on the issues, but Fulbright resented Bumpers's decision to run. At one point during the campaign, Fulbright accused Bumpers of being pro-gun control based on a rather innocuous proclamation he had signed opposing hunting overkill. Archie had been the prime mover behind the proclamation supporting an animal rights group, and he had it signed either by the signing machine or by his own expert imitation of Bumpers's signature. It fell to me and Charlie Gregory, later United States Marshall, to rush around the Second Congressional District and hand out photographs of Bumpers on a duck hunt holding one dead duck in his grip. Of such things, victories are made.

One memorable encounter for me was when I stood in for Bumpers and debated Betty Fulbright, the senator's wife, at Hall High School in Little Rock. Betty, who was elegant and met people well, was an excellent campaigner, but she could not hide her bitterness that Bumpers would challenge her husband, a principled world leader. She was regal in appearance and articulate in her remarks but you sensed that she was somewhat uncomfortable having to debate a Bumpers aide in a high school library. She might have also had a sense that the campaign was not going well for her side. After election day and the sobering defeat, it was said that Fulbright's pollsters hid the bad news from him, and undoubtedly her, during the campaign.

During the Fulbright race, the Bumpers staff would wind up most nights at the Tracks Inn, a bar located on the basement floor of Union Station in Little Rock. There were many escapades. Probably the most memorable was professorial Richard Arnold leaping to the top of a table and dancing. Henceforth, he was known as the Dancing Bear.

But what really changed my life in late spring 1974 was not campaign related. It had to do with Charlotte's health. She had not gotten pregnant after nine years of trying. Most of our friends were having children, and something was definitely wrong and getting worse. Charlotte had lost weight, was in constant back pain, and was having chronic kidney infections. Local physicians had no answers, and one ob-gyn said it was all "just mental." It was frustrating and harder on Charlotte, who desperately wanted a child.

During a visit with friends in Houston, her mother had learned about a renowned fertility specialist, Dr. Robert Franklin. We both agreed that she needed to go see him as soon as possible. Charlotte made a cold call directly to his office and miraculously he agreed to see her with no referral in just two weeks. The local ob-gyn refused to send any of her records.

Charlotte's examination and subsequent laparoscope revealed she had a critical case of endometriosis. Two months later immediately following five and half hours of laser surgery, an exhausted Dr. Franklin commented it was one of two worst cases of endometriosis he had seen to date. He was able to restore only one ovary by patching it together. He also saved her left kidney, which had been severely compromised by the disease. He surmised she would have lost total use of the kidney within six months. With fingers crossed he gave us a 30 percent chance of a pregnancy.

At the behest of his mother, Kula Kumpuris, Dr. Drew Kumpuris held Charlotte's hand following the surgery. Drew was from Little Rock and was chief medical resident in cardiology at Baylor. He would later figure prominently in our family's future. Charlotte indeed became pregnant in 1976, and our son, Stuart, would marry Drew's daughter, Victoria, in 2003. They now have two perfect children, Annabel, 14, and Banks, 11.

Bumpers eventually won the Democratic primary against Fulbright on May 29, 1974, by a margin of almost two to one (Photograph 10). I would later discover that that was his lead before the primary election even began, but in 1974 polls were not common knowledge as they are today. In retrospect, only Deloss Walker, Bumpers, and probably Archie Schaffer knew about the favorable polls before the primary. Bumpers always did contend that Fulbright was extremely vulnerable because of his anti-Vietnam stance and that he could have been defeated in the primary by a radical segregationist like Justice Jim Johnson. After all, Johnson had only lost to Fulbright in 1968 by 30,000 votes.

CHAPTER 12

Washington

Moving to Washington as a Senate aide, assuming I got the offer from Bumpers, was not my first choice. There was an opening on the Public Service Commission, which regulated Arkansas utilities, and I thought that would be a plum appointment and a jump-start to a career in utility work in Arkansas. I went to visit Bumpers about the position. Unfortunately, there had been a newspaper article about my being an aspirant for that job, which, I am sure, did not help my cause with Bumpers. When I told him what I wanted, he said, "Why would you want to do that?" It was then that he said he wanted me to go to Washington as an aide.

Ed Lester, who was an esteemed Little Rock attorney, a mentor to me, and one of Bumpers's campaign leaders, advised me to do it. "Spend two years there and then come back to Conway and run for circuit judge," he said. It was sage advice, which I took only in part. Bumpers appointed a young attorney and my peer, Jerry Jackson, to the PSC, and I went to Washington.

At the end of 1974, the nation's capital was in turmoil. Richard Nixon had resigned the presidency and Vice President Gerald Ford had assumed that position. Democratic warhorses were feeling their oats, Bumpers among them. He was a political force who had now defeated

Orval Faubus, Win Rockefeller, and J. William Fulbright, and was a bona fide member of the New South Club.

The other legislative aides selected to migrate to D.C. were Archie Schaffer and Richard Arnold. Tom McRae did not make the cut, probably of his own choosing. He aspired to be governor of Arkansas, as his great grandfather had been. He would run against Bill Clinton in 1992 and lose.

None of us on Bumpers's staff had reckoned on the animosity the newly elected senator would face in Washington due to his defeat of Fulbright. The Washington establishment viewed Bumpers as a man with vaulting ambition who would not hesitate to savage a true American hero like Fulbright to further his career. Fulbright, after all, had been the much-revered chair of the Senate Foreign Relations Committee and chief skeptic of LBJ's Vietnam strategy. Bumpers, on the other hand, while adroit on the hustings, was untested in the Georgetown drawing rooms of Pamela Harriman and the like. Powerful friends of Fulbright were positioned to make his transition from Little Rock to Washington very painful indeed. Though Fulbright himself was initially standoffish upon Bumpers's arrival, his top aide, Lee Williams, did all that he could to assist Archie, Richard, and me to acclimate.

As senior staff, we all had to get top secret security clearances. I had gotten mine in the first two weeks, and Richard wanted to know what it involved. I told him and mentioned that Archie had his clearance. Richard thought about that a moment. Archie had led a more adventuresome life in the sixties and seventies than the two of us combined, and Richard concluded, "If Archie had his, there was nothing to worry about." It turned out that he was correct.

Bumpers's best friends in the Senate that first two years were Gary Hart of Colorado, John Culver of Iowa, and Wendell Ford of Kentucky. They all had an irreverent sense of humor and were unafraid to poke a stick in the eye of the Democratic establishment, like Robert Byrd of West Virginia, who was vying for chair of the Senate Democratic Caucus. "I got the votes, Dale," Byrd said to Bumpers on one occasion, clicking his cigarette lighter as he asked for Bumpers's vote. Bumpers did not support him and later laughed about him and his solicitation. But Byrd won.

It was established procedure for Senate aides to sit beside the senator they worked for in small chairs on the Senate floor so they could discuss the legislation being debated. I was so positioned one afternoon during a debate on a bill that I had worked on when Bumpers yelled out to John Culver, a couple of aisles in front of him, "I'm voting with the Neanderthals today." The problem was some of those conservative Democrats, or "Neanderthals" as Bumpers had dubbed them, were sitting all around us. It was all part of Bumpers's problematic personality.

At times the staff would let down, especially if the senator had left the office and it was Friday afternoon. Beer and wine would find their way into the office, and shenanigans would ensue. Archie attempted to go down the mail chute on one such occasion.

One Friday was especially memorable. The staff was caught with its proverbial pants down by a delegation from the Arkansas Baptist Federation. With beer cans and wine bottles littering the office premises and Bumpers gone, it was hard to cover up. The delegates were polite but did not stay long. When Bumpers found out about it he was not amused. Archie, the nephew, was the whipping boy for Bumpers, which was fine with us, and Archie heard about it loud and clear. Bumpers called Archie "Spike" and reamed him out Monday morning. But it was a dance they both knew well, and their relationship was quickly mended and back to normal.

The retaliation against Bumpers in the Senate was to come in many forms. Perhaps the biggest slight, in his mind, came with committee assignments. Bumpers wanted the Interior Committee, which at the time encompassed the environment, natural forests, and federal land protection. He got that, but he also wanted Armed Services or Foreign Affairs. Instead, he got Aeronautical and Space Sciences, which he believed was a slap in the face. His interest in space travel was nil, and one day, when whining about the assignment, Senator Hubert Humphrey took him aside and began to explain, in his Happy Warrior fashion, all the exciting programs and opportunities the Space Committee offered.

"Gosh, Dale, you have Landsat for agriculture. The space flights. Potential Mars exploration. Ozone depletion. The possibilities are endless." Bumpers was not mollified.

Gradually, though, he became more enamored of the Space Committee work. Ozone depletion, climate change, surveillance by satellite, and joint space flights with the Soviet Union (Apollo-Soyuz) gave him platforms to explore and intellectual stimulus. Richard was assigned to the Interior Committee work, and my work was the Space Committee, which I enjoyed from the beginning, including a trip to Cape Kennedy to see the first Apollo-Soyuz launch. The takeoff struck me as perfect visual symmetry (Photograph 11).

I would also brief Bumpers on issues involving armed services, like the future of the controversial B-1 bomber, which Bumpers strongly opposed. The Air Force championed it. This led to my being flown by the Air Force brass with other aides to certain military bases like NORAD in Colorado Springs, Colorado, and Omaha, Nebraska, where the Big ICBM board was located. It was really blatant lobbying by the Air Force, but instructive and interesting, nonetheless.

Senate aides were treated like royalty. I drafted an op-ed piece for the *Washington Post* on the lobbying effort of Senate staffers. I showed it to Bumpers before submitting it, and he questioned why I wanted to do that. That was my answer. In my heart of hearts, I knew he thought I was stirring the pot, and he did not like it. In truth, I think I was trying to show my independence, but I never sent the article in to the *Post*.

Apart from his work on ozone depletion, the one piece of legislation Bumpers was known for in his first two years on the Hill was "Right Turn on Red." This legislative brainstorm had its birth as an energy saving bill. The idea was waiting at a red light used gasoline, where a right turn, assuming no traffic, would conserve it. This epiphany came to Bumpers one day while waiting at a stop light, which I told a reporter for *The Wall Street Journal*. The resulting story was on the *Journal's* front page, quoting me. Bumpers was not pleased though it was a good write up.

Right turn on red is still used around the country and has indeed conserved energy. Some, though, have raised questions about how substantive this act was. In my writing days after my return to Little Rock from Washington, I had occasion to interview Hillary Clinton about Bumper's potential race for president in the 1980s. Hillary's comments were: "What's he done as Senator? Right Turn on Red?" she smirked. It was obviously not significant in her judgment.

Work on the Hill in 1975 and 1976 was exciting, but living in Washington was an exhilarating experience as well. Charlotte and I found a house to rent on Quebec Street in Spring Valley, three blocks from Massachusetts Avenue. It was a sizable two-story brick home with a basement and groomed backyard. Richard Arnold lived close by, and every morning he would pick me up in his maroon Lincoln Continental, and we would make the trip down Massachusetts Avenue, the Rock Creek Parkway, and then Constitution Avenue to the Hill.

In the process, Richard and I discussed a myriad of issues and became even closer friends. Those discussions involving literature, politics, the Episcopal Church, and our respective backgrounds kept us both sane. When I turned thirty-five, that morning we both quoted the opening lines of Dante's *Divine Comedy* about my being in the middle of my life in front of Martha Jones (Mason) who was living with Charlotte and me at the time. Richard, however, quoted the lines in the original Italian. We also witnessed firsthand the demise of the Shah of Iran as we passed the Iranian Embassy on Massachusetts Avenue. Demonstrations abounded. We knew a coup was imminent.

One morning as we drove to the Hill, Richard asked: "Bob, do you know what today is?" I answered no. He said, "It's the day the statute of limitations ran on everything to do with the Fulbright campaign." That included any campaign or fundraising activities. We slapped hands in a high five celebration. "There is a God," I muttered.

Like most people, I had the highest respect for Richard. Unhappily, though, he was a largely ineffective political candidate. He had already lost two races for Congress in 1966 and 1972, and his quest to be a United States senator like his maternal grandfather, John Morris

Sheppard, seemed increasingly remote. But he wisely hitched his wagon to a judiciary star with Bumpers as his advocate, and he would have ultimately been appointed to the United States Supreme Court had cancer not intervened. As it was, he was appointed to the federal district court and later served as Chief Judge of the Eighth Circuit Court of Appeals.

While I toiled on the Hill, Charlotte had an active social life with old and new friends and an urge to drink in all of Washington. She took particular advantage of the vibrant art scene and the D.C. art galleries. The Smithsonian and Corcoran museums offered stimulating programs and unique opportunities to meet leading artists in their working environments.

Washington definitely became home for Charlotte and me, and we greatly valued the easy access to New York. But working on the Hill eventually began to lose its luster. In 1976, Bumpers was no longer talked about as a serious presidential contender. For one reason, Jimmy Carter had a two-year head start since serving as governor of Georgia. He and his staff had devoted themselves full time to organizing a national campaign. His staff was highly capable. Most were holdovers from the Georgia governor's office, like Hamilton Jordan, Frank Moore, and Jody Powell.

Bumpers had Richard, Archie, and me, fresh off a senate race but woefully behind as far as any sort of presidential run. One day at lunch, Richard said, half tongue in cheek, "Bob, you take Tennessee, Kentucky, and North Carolina. That leaves only forty-seven states to go."

Ann Pincus, wife of Walter Pincus of *The Washington Post,* who was a good friend and a habitué of the Georgetown cocktail circuit, had a different perspective: "Dale was thought to be too slick by a half." But I also believed I was not being used enough and began looking around for other opportunities. I even wrote to Jack Watson of Carter's transition team in 1976, applying for a job in the new administration. No luck.

Carter was elected president on November 2, 1976. But that was far from the most noteworthy event that happened to me that day. Stuart Laidlaw Brown was born at Georgetown Hospital at 9:58 a.m. –

the true miracle baby. Charlotte and I had dutifully practiced Lamaze, but when labor began I quickly learned that I was not the real coach or as indispensable as the nurse. However, I was front and center for the delivery. His godmother and Charlotte's first cousin, Martha Jones (Mason), was anxiously waiting the news in the patient guest area armed with champagne and *The Book of Common Prayer*. She had somehow convincingly managed a blue light police escort to the hospital in the early morning hours when she was stopped for speeding on her way from Alexandria, Virginia. I attributed her skills of persuasion to her Virginia law school training, where she was in her first year. Seeing and participating in the birth of my son ranks at the top of my experiences on this earth.

But the date presented a major problem. It was Election Day, and no alcohol could be served in Washington restaurants until the polls closed at 7 p.m., which was at least an hour after we arrived to eat. My mother-in-law, Anne Banks, who had flown up from Little Rock after Charlotte went into labor, was fit to be tied at the restaurant, Le Steak, in Georgetown. She promised the waiter everything but eternal life to serve us a celebratory drink. He remained unmoved, so Martha, Anne, and I went without. When the drinks finally came, we made certain – with multiple toasts – that the entire restaurant knew about Stuart's miracle birth. Stuart would return to Washington twenty-two years later to serve as an intern in the Clinton White House under the guidance of Capricia Marshall, social secretary to the president (Photograph 12).

Another election of significance in my life also occurred on November 2. My old friend and attorney general, Jim Guy Tucker, was elected to Congress for central Arkansas, the Second District, and he needed a staff. I was the perfect person to select it and head up his office because I knew both Washington and Arkansas politics. Tucker had been promised a seat on the prestigious Ways and Means Committee chaired by the venerable Wilbur Mills of Kensett for several decades. Mills had resigned in disgrace from the House because of his antics related to alcohol consumption and stripper Fannie Fox, and Tucker had been elected to succeed him. The quid pro quo for the Ways and Means seat, allegedly, was Tucker's promise not to run for the Senate when Senator John McClellan died. McClellan's death seemed imminent. At least two other Arkansas politicians in addition to Tucker wanted that seat – Governor David Pryor and now newly elected Attorney General Bill Clinton.

My tenure with Dale Bumpers had been for two and a half years in the governor's office and two years in the Senate. It would be hard to leave him. But Tucker was an exciting politician full of elan, and I would be in charge of the office. Moreover, no one really believed Tucker would be content to remain a congressman. A Senate seat was too enticing, and, after Fulbright's and McClellan's long tenures, open Senate seats were considered rarities. I factored in a Senate race in making my decision. Tucker made the request, and I accepted.

CHAPTER 13

Congressman Jim Guy Tucker

My decision made, I went to tell Bumpers that Tucker wanted me to be his Gene Goss. It was a reference to Wilbur Mills' former all-purpose and very talented aide. Bumpers laughed and wished me luck. He would later say, jokingly, after thirty years had passed, that after I went to work for Tucker, he never saw me again.

My next visit was to Wilbur Mills to ask him for advice. The visit was not what I expected. Mills appeared very uncomfortable, even defensive. I wanted to talk about the transition between the Mills and Tucker offices, but that's not really what he wanted to discuss.

"You know alcoholism is a disease," he suddenly blurted out. "It's a sickness," he continued, peering down at me over his glasses. He knew about my father's work with Alcoholics Anonymous, like with a well-respected car dealer in Little Rock. Mills said the man could barely hold a coffee cup on a saucer because of his shaking hands when he was in the throes of alcohol. My father got him into AA and probably saved his life, Mills said. He was very respectful and complimentary of Dad's work, no doubt equating his circumstances to those of the car dealer's. It was a connecting point for Mills and me, and our conversation became much easier. At the end, we shook hands warmly, and the congressman offered me every courtesy during the transition.

But catastrophic change was in the air on a different front. We had rented our house on Quebec Street, in the posh Spring Valley section of Washington, from Brandon Grove, the charge d'affaires of the first American ambassador to East Germany, John Sherman Cooper. Grove appeared unannounced on our doorstep right before Christmas 1976 and said he wanted the house back in thirty days and the lease gave him that right. I said no and referred to my newborn son and my nesting, new mother wife. He stalked off, and I was later served with eviction papers. I lawyered up and was able to delay the ouster by several months on the basis that a thirty-day eviction under the lease was fundamentally unfair and violated D.C. regulations, which were decidedly pro tenant. Eventually, even my lawyer turned on me and suggested that it was time for me to vacate.

In the interim, with the help of Ann Pincus, Charlotte and I found a new house on 29th Street between P and Q streets in Georgetown – three stories and a basement and about twenty-five feet wide. It proved to be the perfect move and neighborhood.

I set in motion a move from Quebec Street to Georgetown. First, I rented a truck and persuaded Tucker's staff and other friends to help in the physical move of furniture and books. It was not the smoothest operation, but it was successful. At one point, my good friend T. Martin Davis and I were struggling to wedge a mattress through a railing and balustrade on the third floor. My mother, the good bishop's wife, who was visiting, decided her greatest assistance would be to sit in the corner and pray, while we cursed. Her prayers were answered, and we pushed the mattress through.

Our Georgetown row house was entirely satisfactory. We had acquired yet another new member of the family, a black-and-white Springer Spaniel we named Quincy that we kept at times in the small courtyard in front of the house secured by a wrought iron fence and gate (Photograph 13).

Former Nixon Secretary of State Henry Kissinger lived around the corner from us, and he and his wife, Nancy, had a retriever named Tyler. Quincy and Tyler, mildly put, disliked each other intensely, and, when a Kissinger employee walked Tyler by our house, Quincy, from the courtyard, and Tyler, on the sidewalk, would engage in fierce growls and barking. You knew that if the dogs were free to attack, it would be full fanged war.

Charlotte and I celebrated my birthday with many toasts on June 30, 1977, and after we got home to 29th Street late that night, I paid the babysitter and Charlotte volunteered to walk Quincy. I went to bed on the third floor and then heard a huge commotion on the street. When Charlotte came to bed, I asked her if she had heard the noise. It was then she regaled me with the Quincy-Tyler story.

Walking Quincy, alone on the street, she had decided to take him off the lead, whereupon Henry Kissinger, Nancy, Tyler, and a Secret Service officer rounded the corner. Quincy did not hesitate but charged across the street and attacked Tyler. As Charlotte describes it, she saw her whole life pass in front of her. She too rushed across the street and into the fray, trying to pull Quincy out of the fight.

"Get your dog. Get your dog," Kissinger bellowed, but did nothing to assist. Nor did Nancy or the agent.

Finally, Charlotte got the collar and pulled Quincy away as the Kissinger threesome goose stepped away. Where had the vaunted Kissinger diplomacy gone? Nancy did turn around and said to a bedraggled Charlotte, "It wasn't entirely your fault."

***

It was the seventies on the Hill in Washington, D.C., but the social life among staffers and even some bosses was in high gear. Lobbyists' parties abounded most weekday nights and work on the Hill began about 10:00 a.m. Attractive women staffers found themselves invited to parties by offices across the Hill. One of Tucker's staffers who was especially statuesque was in demand for parties in other offices after work hours. She was offended, but no one thought too much about it. Only if a salon's mistress was a paid staffer with not too much to do other than be "available" for the congressman did it become newsworthy.

Life in the Tucker office was offbeat and exciting, and Tucker was a dynamo of self-promotion and political maneuvering. He was quickly a factor on the Ways and Means Committee, even as a freshman. In a precarious move, he offered an amendment to increase Social Security taxes to better the solvency of the program. It was the third rail for a politician and would later come back to haunt him.

Tucker's sister, Carol Foreman, worked in the Jimmy Carter administration with the Agriculture Department and oversaw certain matters like poultry. Her contacts with the Carter people facilitated Tucker's ability to pull together a Sunday one-on-one interview program for Arkansas television with members of the Carter cabinet like Cyrus Vance (Secretary of State), Jim Schlesinger (Secretary of Energy), Ernest Green (Little Rock Nine Member and Assistant Secretary of Labor) and so forth.

The program was a real coup for Tucker and enhanced his reputation in Arkansas as a Washington player. I would later realize, though, that intelligence and effectiveness are not the most important qualities for a politician to have in the public's mind. Likability is far and away the most important trait to have. David Pryor and Ray Thornton, who would eventually challenge Tucker for the open Senate seat, were liked by just about everyone. Tucker was respected but, in some quarters, begrudgingly so.

Senator John McClellan died in early 1977, and Governor David Pryor had already appointed the talented Kaneaster Hodges to fill out the two years remaining on McClellan's term. Hodges, a Princeton grad, Methodist minister, and Newport lawyer and farmer, was destined to become close friends with Jimmy Carter. Joint duck hunts in Arkansas solidified the relationship, as Kaneaster and his wife, Lindley, became fixtures on the Washington social scene. As an appointed senator, Kaneaster could not succeed himself as an elected senator. Personable as he was, Kaneaster befriended every Arkansan on the Hill.

For me, the handwriting was on the wall, and I knew my time in Washington was coming to a close for several reasons. As Ed Lester had advised, stay only two years, and I was approaching three. If I remained in Washington, my currency would be as a lobbyist, which did not inspire me at all. What did inspire me was creative writing, and particularly a novel based on the sandbar rape case I had prosecuted in 1971. I wrote the first draft of the novel during my time in Washington.

While in Washington, I learned that Johnswood, the historic home of John Gould Fletcher and Charlie May Simon, was on the market after her death in 1977. Fletcher, of course, had won the Pulitzer Prize for poetry, and Simon was a celebrated writer herself, having authored novels, children's books, and biographies of religious figures like Albert Schweitzer (*All Men Are Brothers*). The history and charm of Johnswood appealed to both Charlotte and me, though substantial renovation and the addition of a master bedroom were required. The house had been built in 1941, and Fletcher committed suicide by drowning in a lake just off the property in 1950. At the behest of John Haley, a lawyer who owned the adjoining land, we made a joint bid on the nine acres that comprised the tract and was part of the Simon estate. We were the high bid, and Charlotte and I would eventually take over five acres of the tract with the house named Johnswood (Photograph 14).

But that was after the 1978 senate race between Pryor and Tucker (Photograph 15). Pryor had been governor of the state for over three years and congressman for six years before that. He was, as already mentioned, well known and well liked with a multitude of friends. Tucker had been an active prosecutor and attorney general and had many admirers but also many enemies, including Bill Clinton.

For one thing, Tucker and Clinton were too much alike. Handsome and charismatic, they were both educated in Ivy League schools and represented the next generation of political leaders. Prognosticators predicted one or the other would become president of the United States, and, of course, that is exactly what occurred. Their rivalry caused an uneasiness between the two. Clinton had better national contacts and had kept a rolodex of helpful people all his life. For example, when George McGovern needed state coordinators for his campaign for president in 1972, Clinton was selected to oversee Texas and Arkansas. Tucker got South Dakota.

What ultimately pulled me back to Little Rock was Tucker's run for the United States Senate and my eagerness to put down permanent stakes at Johnswood. Charlotte and I left Washington in early 1978, and this time used a credible moving van service. The night after our row house was empty, we held an Empty House Party with an invitation crafted by advertising executive and good friend Jim Johnson, showing a cartoon of a naked couple in a naked living room representing Charlotte and me (Photograph 16). The party was a huge success with friends from the Hill, the press, and new friends like Richard Fisher, who lived on the same street and had a young child, Anders, who was Stuart's age. Richard would later become president of the Federal Reserve Bank of Dallas.

We loaded into the car the next morning for the drive back to Arkansas. Charlotte was in tears. She had cried when we left Little Rock for Washington. Now she wept as we exited our home three and a half years later. Stuart and Quincy were oblivious but glad to be in a car moving. However, we had no home awaiting us in Little Rock in February 1978. We had sold our house on Centerwood Road to help with the purchase of Johnswood, which was undergoing a complete overhaul. Plus, we were the advance guard. The van with all our furniture was in transit.

We finally hit upon my mother-in-law's house on Beverly Place in Little Rock as a place to light. Anne Banks was a true sport. She put up with our furniture crammed into every nook and cranny, Charlotte and me, her grandson, Stuart, and a dog. At one point Charlotte decided to throw me out of the crowded house over some minor grievance. I remember my suitcases bouncing down the front porch steps. My solution was to move in with an old friend, and later bankruptcy judge, Bobby Fussell. The Fussell guest room was well-known as a home away from home for many strays.

The Democratic Primary in 1978 was a three-man race between Tucker, Pryor, and Thornton, and it was not a particularly nice affair. My good friend Archie Schaffer served as Thornton's campaign manager and I was Tucker's. Thornton, who had replaced Pryor in the United States House of Representatives when Pryor became governor, was the nephew of Witt and Jack Stephens, the brothers who were icons in natural gas production, utilities, and investment banking. Witt

Stephens, in particular, enjoyed politics and could call in many chits from clients and friends on Thornton's behalf.

The result of the preferential primary was an almost even percentage for the three candidates of one-third each. Tucker, however, eked out a victory over Thornton, and Pryor and Tucker headed for the runoff.

What was lacking in the Tucker campaign were representatives of the power structure in Arkansas. Buddy Benafield, the farmer and heavy equipment dealer from England, Arkansas, qualified as one, and he was a close advisor of Tucker's. There were also a few disgruntled McClellan supporters who still faulted Pryor for his brash, unsuccessful race against McClellan in 1972. But these were not enough.

Pryor went for broke in the primary. He hired Dick Morris to coordinate his message. Morris was a Republican and noted mudslinger who set about devising a media strategy around Tucker's missed votes in the House of Representatives due to campaigning and his efforts to make the Social Security fund solvent by increasing payroll taxes. This fed into Morris's efforts to paint Tucker as a "liberal" who was pro labor and too progressive on issues that were distasteful to the Arkansas electorate.

One time, when Tucker was fed up with the liberal tag, he pushed back to a reporter – "Okay, I believe in equal rights for Blacks and fair wages. What else makes me a liberal?"

In the runoff, Tucker fought fire with fire. His staff had learned of an effort by Pryor's campaign manager, Jack Williams, to influence a vote of the Public Service Commission. Specifically, what was alleged was that Williams had approached one PSC commissioner, John Pick-ett, about voting Witt Stephens's way on a rate increase for Arkansas Louisiana Gas Company. That vote would assure Stephens's support for Pryor in the runoff. One of the leaks was to Ernie Dumas of the *Arkansas Gazette*, who published it. Dumas described the leak as being akin to Deep Throat of Woodward/Bernstein fame.

Williams vehemently denied the accusation. Many political observers thought the story would be fatal to Pryor's campaign, but as it happened the story did not move the election needle one iota, and Pryor won the runoff handily. The lesson learned was that the Arkansas people did not believe David Pryor, who was universally viewed as a good guy, would do such a thing or else viewed the whole kerfuffle as just politics.

One other factor that benefited Pryor was that Clinton, who had won the governor's race without a runoff in the presidential primary, was free to encourage his supporters during the two-week runoff period to vote for Pryor. Again, the old Tucker/Clinton feud had reared its ugly head.

CHAPTER 14

Picking Up the Pieces

The Democratic primary for the United States Senate seat ended in May 1978 with David Pryor the winner. He would go on to defeat Republican candidate Tom Kelly in November, and Tucker and I went our separate ways. Tucker began a stint teaching at the University of Arkansas at Little Rock and then joined the Mitchell law firm in Little Rock. I joined my old friend, Fred Harrison, in a two-man partnership we named Harrison and Brown, P.A.

Though a year younger, I met Fred when I first moved to Little Rock in 1955. Because I was new and not a master of the .22 caliber rifle, I was accused by Fred of wounding him in the foot down at the rock quarry outside of Little Rock one Saturday afternoon. He had been hit by a stray shot, and I was the most likely culprit since I had been down at the quarry during the suspect time with other friends. Later, Fred and I would see each other during college and law school breaks in Little Rock and became close friends.

Fred was once asked what the specialty of our law firm was, and his quick response was, "It's a grab ass practice." That was not completely true. Fred had clients from his previous practice with his now deceased father-in-law, Tom Downie, who had been Governor Winthrop Rockefeller's personal counsel. And I developed a litigation practice that eventually focused on bankruptcy law.

I also wrote articles and profiles of Arkansas leaders for the *Arkansas Times* monthly magazine at the request of its editor, Bill Terry. Over the next decade, my articles included rating the members of the Arkansas congressional delegation in terms of effectiveness, and profiles of FedEx's CEO Fred Smith, Arkla Gas President Sheffield Nelson, and Governor Frank White. Eventually, I was made a contributing editor of the *Arkansas Times*. I also wrote articles for *Arkansas Business* and *The Arkansas Lawyer*, as well as op-ed pieces for the *Arkansas Gazette.*

During the 80s, Charlotte returned to Poe Travel as the office manager. Stuart was in public schools through the ninth grade and began an active sports program that included soccer and basketball. He had a particular talent for tennis and spent many hours training on the courts of the Little Rock Racquet Club. We were hands-on tennis parents, chaperoning him and his teammates to tournaments around the state and beyond. His last three years of secondary school education were at Woodberry Forest School in Orange, Virginia, where his maternal grandfather and great uncle had attended. There he continued to excel on the tennis team, making the All-Virginia Prep League.

In the mid-80s, my law partner, Fred Harrison, went to work as legal counsel for the University of Arkansas system at the request of its president, who was now Ray Thornton. I became associated with the law firm of Arnold, Grobmyer & Haley, which fed me legal business. It was a fragmented time.

Close college friend and Stuart's godfather from New Orleans, Gerald DeBlois, needed legal representation to buy a psychiatric clinic, Cedarstone, in North Little Rock. That led to a burgeoning practice for me in the certificate-of-need area as I began to represent hospital developers that wanted to locate in Arkansas and had to establish need. It began with converting Cedarstone into a psychiatric hospital, The Bridgeway, followed by The Psychiatric Hospital of Texarkana (Photograph 17).

CHAPTER 15

Travel

Travel has always loomed large in my life with Charlotte, and the 80s were no exception.

On our twentieth wedding anniversary, there was the ten-day cruise through the Bahamas and West Indies on a small French ship, *The Renaissance*, to six ports of call. Because Charlotte was a travel agent, we were given deluxe cabins that came with plush, purple robes for the outdoor swimming pool. They were quite a contrast to the vast majority of white robes. Only the very well-heeled wore these, and we were amused by our instant popularity. We laughingly revealed our true identity to our newfound friends at the trip's conclusion.

The ship managed to run aground off Haiti, which was bad form on the captain's part. It took some hours, but the tide eventually rescued us. Voodoo drums heard offshore added some excitement to the long delay. An elderly American naval officer who was a passenger on the cruise said that in his day such an error would have resulted in the "bloody miscreant" being keelhauled. The six remaining ports of call made up for it.

The second trip was to the Soviet Union, which Charlotte and I took separately. Charlotte went earlier with three Poe Travel agent friends. My trip was a tad more interesting because I was the tour guide through Poe Travel for eleven Arkansans. Plus, it was in the summer and warmer. Having said that, Charlotte was in Leningrad (St. Petersburg) in the dead of winter, and the Neva River was frozen. She and friends were able to ride a sleigh across the ice.

In the summer of 1987, Soviet leader Mikhail Gorbachev was implementing economic reforms (perestroika) and about to embark on more openness in government (glasnost). But for purposes of our tour in Russia, it was the old Soviet Union. We had "In Tourist" guides furnished by the Soviet Union. We could not take photographs of strategic sites like train stations, and we could not wander away on our own. Plus, I knew our hotel telephones in Moscow and St. Petersburg were bugged.

We saw the sites, of course. At one point our guide asked me confidentially what had really happened to the Tsar Nicholas II and his family. She had heard that they were still alive in South America. I quickly disabused her of that and told her they were murdered. At the State Hermitage Museum in St. Petersburg, she did not show us the French Impressionists paintings because the work was considered frivolous and of no Marxist significance. We then traveled to Warsaw from Moscow on Swiss Air. I was overjoyed. We had scrambled eggs and rolls on the flight for breakfast.

I wrote an op-ed piece for the *Gazette* upon my return, arguing that despite Gorbachev, the Soviet Union was not as open as we might think. Boy was I wrong. Within two years, the Berlin Wall was down, and the Soviet Union was no more.

Photo1: The author at age 65 in Little Rock and at age 6 in Waco.
(Courtesy of the David Pryor Center for Oral History)

Photo 2: Boy Scout Honor Guard for Eisenhower with the author
at St. Paul's Episcopal Church, May 9, 1954.

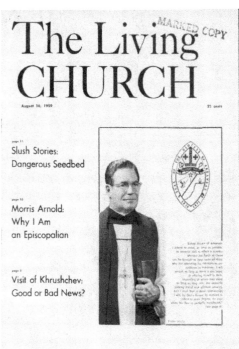

Photo 3: The Brown family with the author in Richmond before moving to Little Rock, circa 1955.

Photo 4: Robert R. Brown, the author's father, on the cover of *The Living Church* for taking a stand on desegregation during the Little Rock crisis.

Photo 5: The Banks's home in Fordyce where Charlotte grew up.

It's **Anne Jones Banks'** energy, enthusiasm and common sense that inspire her daughter **Charlotte Brown**. Charlotte describes her 87-year-old mother as "the ultimate positive thinker" who cares deeply about her family and friends.

"Nothing brings her more pleasure than daily doing something thoughtful or kind for her family or one of her host of friends," Charlotte said. Anne also keeps a busy social schedule with weekly exercise classes, travel and occasional trips around the dance floor. "Mother is always making our lives better and definitely more interesting and fun." Charlotte said.

Photo 6: Charlotte and her mother, Anne Jones Banks.

Photo 7: Charlotte's engagement picture, 1965.

Photo 8: The author as legal aide to Governor Dale Bumpers in the governor's office, circa 1973.

Photo 9: Christmas party at the Governor's Mansion in 1973
with Gov. Dale Bumpers, Betty Bumpers, Charlotte, and the author.

Photo 10: Dale Bumpers, Betty Bumpers, and the campaign staff the day after
he defeated J. William Fulbright for the U.S. Senate in 1974.
The staff includes Richard Arnold, Archie Schaffer, and the author.

Photo 11: Senator Bumpers and an astronaut at NASA with the author and Archie Schaffer, 1976

To Charlotte and Bob
With best wishes, *welcome!* Bill Clinton

Photo 12: President Bill Clinton, Stuart, the author, and Charlotte in the Oval Office, 1995.

Photo 13: The author, Stuart, Charlotte, and Quincy (the Springer Spaniel)
in the garden of our Georgetown home, 1977.

You are invited to an extremely Open House on February 28 at around 7:30.
1528 29th Street N.W. (Between P & Q). Come make some echos echos echos ....
338-6326 if Regretting.

Photo 14: The "Empty House" party invitation for February 28, 1977,
the night before the author and family left Washington. (Credit: Jim Johnson)

Photo 15: Johnswood, purchased in 1978 by the author and Charlotte, and their home for 45 years.

Photo 16: Jim Guy and Betty Tucker announcing his candidacy for the U.S. Senate, 1978.

Photo 17: The groundbreaking for the Bridgeway Psychiatric Hospital with Gerald DeBlois, the author, Senator Ben Allen, and Bob Smith.

Photo 18: The author's campaign button, palm card, and brochure for Arkansas Supreme Court race, 1990.

Photo 19: Administrative assistant Pat Tucker, the author,
and law clerks Lisa Peters and Bill Jones, 1991.

Photo 20: Members of the Arkansas Supreme Court, including the author,
in front of the Justice Building, early 2000s.

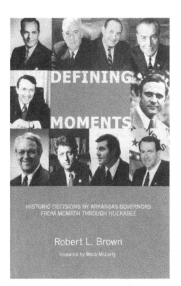

Photo 21: *Defining Moments*, by the author, discusses pivotal decisions made by Arkansas governors from McMath to Huckabee. It was published in 2010.

Photo 22: *The Second Crisis of Little Rock*, a report by the author, looked back on school desegregation crisis. It was published by the Rockefeller Foundation thirty years after the integration of Little Rock Central High School.

Photo 23: Charlie May Simon Fletcher and John Gould Fletcher, who built Johnswood in 1941.

Photo 24: Stuart and Victoria after he proposed marriage at La Grenouille restaurant in New York in 2002.

Photo 25: Banks and Annabel, grandchildren par excellence, in 2021.

Photo 26: Author at work.

Photo 27: Author and Charlotte relaxed in retirement in Cashiers, 2021. (Credit Jim Theus)

CHAPTER 16

A Seed is Planted

Toward the end of the decade, a justice on the Arkansas Supreme Court, Steele Hays, asked me, "Why don't you run for the Supreme Court? Three seats are opening up." I had just done a cover piece on court legend Justice George Rose Smith for *The Arkansas Lawyer,* January 1987, upon his retirement and knew the inner workings of the court well. Justice Smith had devised a system for case assignments and the drafting of legal briefs that is still in use today.

Steele Hays had planted a seed, and I began to think more and more about a statewide race for the Supreme Court. Because I had worked in statewide campaigns for Dale Bumpers and Jim Guy Tucker, I knew how to do it. And politics was intoxicating stuff. Plus, as a Supreme Court justice, I would have a seat at the table, figuratively speaking, and could make a difference.

It would be a bold move because I had never run for political office. And yet, public service was very much a part my heritage and makeup. My father had been a bishop, overseeing the Diocese of Arkansas and tended to the needs of his flock. My maternal grandfather had been a Virginia state senator. Dale Bumpers had always trumpeted that politics was a noble profession, and that statement as well as the upfront and professional way that Bumpers practiced his craft influenced me greatly.

My father had once asked me after college to consider the ministry, but I simply did not feel the call to do that. I would make my mark in other ways. Government by way of politics, I believed, was the way for me to do just that. I never viewed politics as a dirty business, although I wasn't naïve about the dark side of the game. It could be a rough and even brutal affair.

Two matters had to be determined immediately. The first was the person I would run against. As it happened, Steele Hays decided to run again for the court, which meant there were two choices: Don Corbin, who was Chief Judge of the Arkansas Court of Appeals and before that a member of the Arkansas House of Representatives, and Judith Rogers, who had been a chancery and probate judge and then a member of the Arkansas Court of Appeals.

My second challenge was to gather a kitchen cabinet to advise me on strategy, which I did early in 1989. The cabinet had great talent: lawyers Henry Hodges and Mark Grobmyer, former Supreme Court Chief Justice Webb Hubbell, former Insurance Commissioner and Bumpers's aide Ark Monroe, and Fred Harrison, who had considerable campaign experience, to name a few.

We first met at the Capital Hotel for breakfast and the question I posed was, "who should my opponent be?" The advice was unanimous – Judith Rogers. Corbin was simply too well liked and Rogers was considered too political, which was a minus for any judge. The decision made, I began selecting key cogs for my machine. I needed a campaign planner, and Mary Dillard, who had worked on issue-related campaigns, fit the bill. She made it clear from the outset that she would plan and give global advice but would not manage the day-to-day operations of the campaign.

A finance person for fundraising came next, and later a media consultant and campaign manager. Mary and I set to work on a media consultant. We flew to Dallas with Charlotte and interviewed Mike Shannon. He was perfect. He had done ads for Bill Richardson's first campaign for Congress in New Mexico. He had also done a very effective campaign spot for a client against an opponent in a state senate race in Texas. That opponent had previously crashed his airplane twice. The spot begins with siren blasts and checkered flags being frantically waved on a runway. Next, a man dives off to the side of the runway as a Cessna crash lands. The punchline to the spot was "if he can't fly a plane safely, how can he represent you in the state senate?" I was sold. I hired Shannon. What he later developed for my campaign was a classic in political advertisement and won awards for its cleverness and effectiveness, including a first place Pollie Award.

Henry Hodges guided me to former Worthen Bank CEO and community leader Ed Penick, his wife's uncle, to head up fundraising. The Penick family were old friends and extremely well respected in the banking community. The campaign manager position was harder to fill. We eventually settled on Libby Smith for the role. She had earned her spurs as office manager for Congressman Jake Pickell of Texas. And she was married to Griffin Smith, who had extraordinary credentials in politics, writing, and the Arkansas legal community. His grandfather had been chief justice of the Arkansas Supreme Court, and he had been a speech writer for President Jimmy Carter. Later, he would be executive editor of the *Arkansas Democrat-Gazette*.

Then it was a matter of Charlotte and me touring the state and developing a statewide organization. The ideal would be to have a principal supporter in most of the seventy-five counties, but at least a solid organization in the twenty most populous counties (Photograph 18).

Charlotte and I looked to three areas for key personnel. First and foremost, there were people I had worked with in the Tucker and Bumpers campaigns. Then, there were the lawyers whom I knew in the Arkansas Bar. And, finally, there were Episcopal church contacts and personal friends. My father, after all, had had his own statewide network as bishop of Arkansas, and I had met many contemporaries at conventions and church camps, as well as many lay people who were leaders in their communities. Charlotte had her own network of business associates and her mother, Anne Banks, was a force of nature with many friends across the state.

There were two concerns, however, with full-time campaigning. The most serious for us was our son, Stuart, who was at the pivotal age of twelve. He needed and deserved full-time parents. Anne, as always, came to our rescue and enthusiastically assumed the important role of third parent for Stuart. And if Charlotte and I were to hit the campaign trail, income from our two jobs would become nonexistent. That is where liquidating investments like Walmart stock came into play. The gifts from family and friends well before the campaign started also played a vital role. It all somehow worked, but with family sacrifices that accompany any political campaign.

I quickly learned by my political peregrinations that the true leadership in Arkansas is not found in Little Rock but out in the state in the smaller cities and communities. That is where a campaign was to be won or lost. I went to county bar meetings, political rallies, churches, livestock auctions, Christmas and July 4th parades, and festivals of every stripe, where I could meet and greet voters and hand out brochures and palm cards. My brochure pictured my golden retriever, which prompted one deputy clerk in the Faulkner County Courthouse to say, "He can't be all bad, he's got a dog."

The truth of the matter is that Charlotte and I thoroughly enjoyed campaigning. We routinely divided our efforts to cover more territory. Charlotte would head off to one of the local festivals to pitch the crowd from the stump. She was often accompanied by supportive friends, like Helen Harrison or Elsa Crocker. Campaign stalwart Sam Ledbetter found himself at the wheel any number of times when it was an evening event. Elsa loves to talk about the time when they were way behind schedule down in lower Arkansas. Charlotte had spent fifteen minutes trying to convince a man to vote for me only to find out he could not vote because he was a convicted felon.

One magnificent idea for our palm cards came from Henry Hodges. He said, "Put the Arkansas Razorbacks football Schedule on the back. People will keep them and put them on their refrigerators." I followed Henry's advice, and the cards were a big hit. I even had separate cards for the Arkansas State Indians (now Red Wolves) schedule. Judith Rogers would quip that it looked like I was running for coach – not the Supreme Court.

I knew from experience that the all-important factor and expense would be my television campaign spots. Mike Shannon developed two, both of which were controversial and highly effective. Before developing his television spots, Shannon did a statewide poll to take the pulse of the electorate. One question was about the ACLU and the impact that a candidate's membership might have on one's vote. Judge Rogers had either been a member or an ACLU sympathizer. I don't remember the poll or being aware of the question in advance. The polling question got out, however, presumably from a Judge Rogers supporter who was called as part of the poll. When my good friend Brownie Ledbetter learned about it she apparently was livid. She wrote me off and supported Judge Rogers. It was passing strange to me, because the ACLU was never raised as an issue in my campaign.

The first television ad touted my experience as a prosecutor in Jim Guy Tucker's office. The spot carried the message that people were fearful of crime, and as a judge I would be tough on criminals. To some, that flew in the face of judicial impartiality.

The second spot was masterful. It opened with a photograph of a newspaper article stating that Judge Rogers had spent $13,000 to order new furniture for her court of appeals office. That included Chippendale chairs. The spot went on to say Judge Rogers believed the furniture would last forever. And then there was the kicker. The voiceover said, "At the rate Judge Rogers uses the furniture, it will last forever." A door opened to her office which was covered with cobwebs. Even the scales of justice were covered. The clear point was she was never there but instead was on vacation, attending judicial conferences, and so forth. We had done opponent research and determined she had missed more than a hundred days of work the previous calendar year. While that statistic was highlighted, the Hawaiian tune, "Aloha" played in the background.

The television ad was devastating. Some friends called to criticize me for going negative. Others thought Chippendale referred to the male strippers. Judge Rogers, when she saw me at a meeting, did a Hawaiian dance, but later called me "dishonest" for the cobweb spot in her own television commercial. But that ad had been well researched, and its facts were accurate. So there was negativity on both sides.

The polls showed the race was tightening, which was exciting. Running against someone with "Judge" in front of her name on the ballot was said to give that person a twenty-five percent advantage. Plus she was much better known than I was. So I needed to fire the jets to catch up, and that was happening.

There was also the Bill Clinton machine that worked for Judge Rogers. That was critically important in the Arkansas Delta which had a large concentration of Black voters and where voter lists were distributed. Clinton's support in the Black community had always been staggeringly high.

Toward the last days of the campaign the telephones were not ringing and things seemed stagnant. The *Arkansas Gazette* had endorsed Judge Rogers and the *Pine Bluff Commercial* had said, "Pay your money and take your choice," which meant it took a walk.

Shannon suggested I run another radio ad to the effect that some of Judge Rogers's vacations were in Las Vegas. The sound of coins cascading down a chute at a slot machine was in the background, suggesting she was gambling. I refused to run the ad.

But I did allow the release of a story that she had been the lawyer for the pornographic film *Deep Throat*, which was shown in North Little Rock. It was true, but as one reporter, Max Brantley, commented to me, even pornographers need legal representation. The news story was very effective and raised more questions about Judge Rogers. That is when you appreciate support from friends. After the story broke, Austin Jennings, senior partner of a major Little Rock law firm (Wright, Lindsey & Jennings), called on a Saturday morning and gave me a much-needed pep talk.

It was coming down to the wire, and it was only then that I realized no one had thought I would win. My family and I always thought I would, but most knowledgeable people did not. We watched election results with friends, and it was nip and tuck. For most of the night, the lead seesawed back and forth, and the race was too close to call. Late election night and into the early morning, friends and supporters spread out into the state to watch votes being counted in courthouses in vital counties to safeguard against voter fraud.

The day after the election, May 29, I was behind by thirty-two votes. That afternoon I was ahead by about one hundred and fifty. Votes were still being counted. This is when Rev. Hezekiah Stewart, a pastor in College Station, told me to go out and "claim the victory," citing scripture. It was the best advice I got, other than Justice Hays's suggestion. I called a press conference and claimed the victory, although the margin was pitifully small.

But that had a psychological impact. People thought I had won, and after the press conference some votes were still being counted and my margin grew to 1,100 votes. Judge Rogers, of course, asked for a recount and that was set to take place at the Pulaski County courthouse the following Saturday, June 2. I had a team of people ready to watch: Bob Ross, Dick Hatfield, Robert Lowry, Fred Harrison, Mark Grobmyer, Henry Hodges, Bruce Bullion, and other close friends and associates.

Interestingly, a few days before the recount I got a telephone call from lawyer Jim Blair of Fayetteville, a principal in Judge Rogers's campaign and fervent friend of the Clintons, saying that if my campaign agreed to pay off Judge Rogers's campaign debt, she would concede. I told him, "No!"

There was also the matter of Clinton. We knew his organization had worked against me and supported Judge Rogers. We also knew Clinton had a Republican opponent in the general election in November – Sheffield Nelson. My people, Mark Grobmyer in particular, let it be known that my organization would support Nelson if Clinton did not stay neutral in the recount. That week before the recount I got a telephone call from Olly Neal, a lawyer from Marianna in the Delta, who would eventually serve on the Arkansas Court of Appeals. He assured me the recount in the Delta counties would be straight. I asked him why he had not supported me in the primary election, and he said I had been shown around Marianna by someone in the Daggett Law Firm, which was the old establishment firm and perceived as not friendly to Black activists. The man who had shown me around was Jimmy Van Dover. Clinton, though, had gotten the message, and I suspected Olly Neal was his peace emissary.

That Saturday morning, my team mobilized in my law office in Center Place just two blocks from the courthouse. Right before the team was to march over en force, I went to the bathroom. Upon emerging, everyone cheered and clapped, which I found rather perplexing. Judge Rogers had called to concede. Great relief washed over us, and the celebration began. The back story is that Judge Rogers had tried to call my home that morning to concede. Stuart, who was asleep on the floor of his room in a sleeping bag, had knocked the phone off the hook. She then called my law office.

My mother and father had been troupers during the campaign. Both had written letters supporting my candidacy to friends and had offered staunch support to Charlotte and me, although I knew that the roughness of the campaign with the hard-hitting TV advertisements was not their cup of tea. At a victory party we had some two weeks later for friends and supporters, they clearly had a good time and were proud of what we all had accomplished.

I was under no illusion that the hurt from Judge Rogers' loss to me easily healed. Indeed, I knew it remained an open wound. She had told Justice Bob Dudley on my court at the annual Bar Association meeting in June 1990, shortly after my election, that her loss was "God's will," which he laughingly recounted to me.

As the fall approached before my swearing in, I called Judge Rogers, who would remain on the Court of Appeals, and invited her to lunch. She agreed, and we ate in a downtown restaurant, which caused some comment from those who saw us because the race was fresh in people's minds. We had always been friends I reminded her, and the race was simply "business." I wanted to be on the court. So did she. To her credit, Judge Rogers was always professional with me after the race. And so it was over.

CHAPTER 17

How Best to Anoint Our Justices?

"REMEMBER: MY NAME IS PURTLE.
IT RHYMES WITH TURTLE."
John Purtle campaigning for the Arkansas Supreme Court

I came to the Arkansas Supreme Court in 1991, five years after Justice John Purtle had been acquitted following a jury trial for conspiracy to commit arson for profit. He was reputed to have had an affair with his legal secretary who was similarly indicted, but she was convicted. Despite the charge and acquittal, Justice Purtle remained on the court three more years before resigning a year early.

He was clearly a blight on the court, especially in the eyes of the straight-laced Justice George Rose Smith, who considered him an abomination. At the same time, Purtle had his defenders. He was a maverick who bucked the system. *The New York Times* featured him in a story in 1990 that echoed that theme and depicted him as an outsider not to the manor born who was a fierce defender of the little guy. His dissenting opinions often sided with the criminal defendants and against the prosecutors and police.

There had earlier been a whiff of scandal associated with Purtle and Chief Justice Richard Adkisson for receiving benefits from a person of dubious reputation. The rumors were denied by both men. In 1984, Adkisson surprised everyone by announcing his retirement at the end of the court's current term. Adkisson was renowned, according to Justice Bob Dudley, for lying on the couch in the conference room during conferences and proclaiming with dramatic emphasis when a harsh decision was made by the court, "There is a whole lot of pain and suffering in this world."

All of this is to say, the image of the Supreme Court had been tarnished, and it gave rise to the old argument that we should choose our justices by gubernatorial appointment rather than popular election. Establishment attorneys in the larger firms seemed more inclined to favor that system.

It has been said that the Brown-Rogers campaign for the Supreme Court, with its rancor and abundant spending ($400,000 by Brown and $265,000 by Rogers), was an excellent reason to change from popular elections to an appointment system. No doubt, my race was a fiercely contested affair where both of us went for broke. When one dissident who favored appointing justices said, "Well, Bob Brown spent too much money," my good friend, Bob Smith, alluding to the closeness of the race, answered, "No, he spent just enough."

The campaign, however, did raise eyebrows and revived the perennial debate of whether having an appointment system for selecting justices for our Supreme Court was preferable to popular elections. I would eventually write a law review article for the *UALR Law Journal* in 1998 entitled "From Whence Cometh Our State Appellate Judges: Popular Election Versus the Missouri Plan," where I endorsed popular elections.

The editor of the *Law Journal* at the UALR Law School at that time was Phoebe Roaf, who was the daughter of Justice Andree Roaf. Justice Roaf had been appointed by Governor Tucker in 1996 to serve a one-year unexpired term on the Supreme Court. She was the first African American woman to be a justice on the court. We were good friends and worked well together. I was never called "Bob" by Andree but always "Brown." Phoebe Roaf later clerked for a federal judge in New Orleans, and then had a higher calling. A lifelong Episcopalian, she went to Virginia Theological Seminary and later was ordained a priest. In 2019, she was ordained and consecrated Episcopal Bishop of the Diocese of West Tennessee and now serves in that role.

At the time of my article on selecting justices, my thought was that Phoebe Roaf would favor appointing justices because of her mother's experience. My article, on the other hand, endorsed selection by popular election. Part of my reasoning was pragmatic. I knew Arkansas at its core was a state steeped in Jacksonian Democracy. Its people wanted a voice in choosing the Supreme Court justices and were not willing to abdicate that role in deference to the governor. Nor did I believe the caliber of appointed justices overall was superior to elected justices. In 1998, when I wrote the article, I mentioned Justice Roaf and Clinton's Secretary of Transportation, Rodney Slater, as two African Americans who were viable candidates for the court.

The Missouri Plan, or Merit Selection as it is sometimes called, initially gained considerable popularity for selecting appellant judges and justices after it was first implemented in Missouri in 1940. Since that time, twenty-four states have adopted that procedure for selecting their Supreme Court justices. The plan provides for a nominating committee, like a Bar Association committee, to recommend a slate of candidates for justice to the governor. The governor then appoints one, and at the next election date that appointed justice stands for election for a full term in a retention election. That candidate has no opponent but appears on the ballot for the voters to say yes or no to a full term for that justice. The alternative plan most used is popular elections with adversarial candidates. This process is used in twenty-two states, including Arkansas. The remaining few states have their legislatures elect their judges or elect them for life terms.

My objection to the Missouri Plan has always been twofold. Initially, it seemed to me to embrace a different kind of politics. What special interests are influencing the nominating committee or governor, for example? Plus, the Missouri Plan entailed a retention election with all an election involves, like raising money and running campaign ads. But to make matters worse, a candidate for retention can be attacked on issues and previous opinions without having an opponent as a foil. With an opponent, the question could be asked to the attacking adversary: "What would you have done in a similar case?"

But there is another corrosive element to Supreme Court elections and that is the money problem.

In 1971, the Supreme Court held in *Buckley v. Valeo* that campaign donations were protected political free speech. Later, contributions would be enshrouded in corporate layers to hide the real donor's identity. This phenomenon would eventually be dubbed "Dark Money." I wrote about the perils of dark money in op-ed articles for the *Arkansas Democrat-Gazette* after my retirement:

> Democracy is defined as government by the people. What could be more damaging to a democracy based on popular elections than secret money buying the elections? As Arkansans, this should appall and deeply offend each and every one of us. The people's right to know who is behind these costly political ads is transcending and overcomes any notion that these clandestine contributors have any superior right to privacy or protected speech.

United States Supreme Court Justice Antonin Scalia, who championed unlimited corporate contributions to nonprofit contributors to political campaigns, strongly advocated transparency from individual givers. He wrote: "Requiring people to stand up in public for their political acts fosters civic courage, without which democracy is doomed."

The United States Supreme Court abetted the dark money problem in *Citizens United v. FEC* in 2010, when it held that contributions from nonprofit 501c corporations were also protected speech no matter how large the amount contributed.

Later, my focus was on false ads in judicial campaigns. It was truly an uphill battle and one that never met with total success, although I was able to raise awareness of the problem. My first journey into the fray was to write an article for the *Arkansas Lawyer* in 2009 entitled

"Toxic Judicial Elections: A Proposed Remedy." Voter guides for judicial elections and truth committees for false and misleading campaign ads were advocated. Following the article, the Arkansas Supreme Court authorized Chief Justice Jim Hannah and me to appear before the Bar Association's Board of Governors to ask for the appointment of a task force to study campaign reform. Initial members were appointed by Bar President Jim Julian, and we were off and running. I served as task force chair.

Over the next months, the task force met eight times with witnesses from Arkansas and other states, where we explored remedies ranging from voter guides to rapid response teams to address immediately outright lies by candidates in advertising. This work came to a halt in August 2010. The *Arkansas Times* weekly newspaper published an article that explored the work of the task force and the problems of lies and big money in judicial campaigns. It focused on the Chamber of Commerce, Republican Party entities, and conservative PACS and concluded they were the primary malefactors in this regard. This was a disaster. The task force had just been labeled a tool of the Democratic Party.

After the *Arkansas Times* article, the Bar Association became skittish about the task force's creation and work and by the end of 2010 had publicly terminated it. For the next five to six years, judicial election reform lay dormant while dark money from undisclosed third-party nonprofit corporations from out of state poured into Arkansas Supreme Court races and usually elected those benefitting.

In 2016, former Justice Annabelle Imber Tuck picked up the torch for judicial reform, and a new board and rapid response team were selected. Again it met with opposition from the Republican Party as being too partisan and as an attempt to curtail free speech.

As this is being written, only a voter's guide posted on a judicial website in Arkansas informing the public about the background of candidates appears to be a viable reform. A second vehicle for reform would be state legislation to mandate disclosure of those paying the dark money for political ads on radio and television. Though legislation was promoted by Representative Clarke Tucker during his term in the

Arkansas House of Representatives to do just that and later by Representative Andrew Collins, it failed to make viable progress. In July 2020, the Internal Revenue Service adopted regulations making disclosure of donors to 501c corporations virtually impossible. So what initially seemed a critically important legislative initiative where all could agree became highly controversial and was eventually abandoned by the Bar Association.

CHAPTER 18

Now It Begins

For the remainder of 1990, I practiced some law but also tried to learn what life as a Supreme Court justice would mean. I had selected my administrative assistant, Pat Gill, who had worked for my law firm. But I needed two law clerks to help with research and memos on cases. I knew full well that blue ribbon law clerks were essential for a successful tenure on the court, and I hired two of the best, after testing the writing and analytical skills of all applicants: Lisa Peters and Bill Jones.

Regretfully, there was no orientation for a new justice. Nothing. The latter part of December 1990, fourteen cases were delivered to my law office to be decided the first week of January 1991. Each case was made up of briefs, that is, legal arguments for affirmance or reversal of the trial court's decision. With the help of my new law clerks, I dove in (Photograph 19).

It officially began at midnight January 1, 1991, when I was sworn in as an associate justice of the Arkansas Supreme Court by Chief Justice Jack Holt in my living room at Johnswood. Charlotte held the Bible with Stuart and close family and friends present. Later at my public swearing in at the Supreme Court courtroom, I received a judicial robe from the Pulaski County Bar Association. Charlotte and Stuart helped robe me. There is something transformative about putting on the robe.

It is a Shazam moment, and you immediately appear to others in a different light.

Though there was no formal orientation, court people were very helpful to me in getting my feet on the ground. I soon realized, though, that the Supreme Court was not the last word in certain categories of cases. The Court of Appeals was the last word, as a practical matter, in major areas of the law – contracts and property, to name two. That made no sense to me, and it violated the spirit of the Arkansas Constitution. But this was a holdover from Justice George Rose Smith's system for the court. The rationale was to reduce the caseload for the Supreme Court.

A second major procedural deficiency was that any case could be orally argued if counsel requested it, even when the issues might be minor in the extreme. On most days for oral arguments, we had at least three – twenty minutes for each side. That was not the optimum use of the court's time.

Still another area of procedure that needed reform was the date we held oral arguments. When I got on the court, it was Monday. That meant weekends were devoted to preparation by the justices, the law clerks, and the attorneys for the parties. Work on Sundays by all involved was *de rigueur*. It ruined everyone's weekends, especially for the justices.

And, finally, many of the cases decided by the Supreme Court should not have been there at all. The issue of law may have already been decided or was not of major significance, or in criminal cases involving more than thirty years of incarceration, could easily have been decided by the Court of Appeals.

What was needed was a complete overhaul of the inner workings of appellate work for the court. That would not take place until seven years later in 1998 with these major changes:

- Oral arguments would occur on Thursday instead of Monday. This was a notable change spearheaded by Chief Justice W.A. "Dub" Arnold.

- Oral arguments for cases would be heard at the court's discretion. Justice David Newbern was instrumental in making this change.

It was the first step in the court becoming a certiorari court, which meant it could decide what cases should be accepted and decided. Next, the Supreme Court announced that it would only decide death cases, matters of first impression in the law, and cases of significant public interest. Everything else would be handled by the Court of Appeals. This, in 1998, completed the transition to a certiorari court. The court would screen cases for those that met one of these criteria and receive case transfers from the Court of Appeals on the same basis. The jurisdiction of the Supreme Court was established accordingly (Photograph 20).

When I got on the court, I knew I was proficient enough to write opinions and do the research. What I was less sure about were the more practical aspects of the court. By that, I mean what would it take to persuade three other justices to join me in a case for a four-person majority? With four votes, Justice Don Corbin would often say, you could do anything. It was true, as I soon found out, and that was the ultimate challenge of every justice. How to get and keep a majority.

* * *

The early nineties were a time of significant upheaval for me. I had entered a new world on the court that demanded major time, focus, and effort. Charlotte had an equally challenging job as development director for the Arkansas Arts Center, where she worked for the immensely creative museum director and curator, Townsend Wolfe.

Both Charlotte and Stuart were sources of joy and pride, but I would become withdrawn, steeped in my work, and rather noncommunicative. Then, both of my parents died; my mother in 1992 and my father in 1994. That left a tremendous void in my family. The truism that you only become an adult when your parents die proved to be exactly correct. With the outpouring of love and affection following their deaths, it was brought home to me once again the significant mark Dad left on the church in race relations and how my mother was beloved.

America was also going through a significant shift. Ronald Reagan and George H.W. Bush had led the country for twelve years. Now the country was restless and yearned for change. Enter Bill Clinton.

Clinton was a flawed long shot for president, and I had watched him for years. He always got my vote, but his strengths and weaknesses were obvious. After his election in 1992, I went to an inauguration party in Washington, D.C., where I met Lauren Bacall and told her I was from Little Rock. "Well, what do you think about our new president?" she asked. I answered that I was proud but that I viewed his election with "some alarm." She was crestfallen but quickly regained her composure. "Don't worry," she said, patting me on the shoulder. "It will be all right."

But it wasn't only Clinton. The country was on the brink of the high-speed computer and the internet age. Instant information and communications. There was also wholesale cultural changes. Sexual identity. An exposed and faulty education system. Crack cocaine and meth. Enter the War on Drugs captured in *Bangin' in Little Rock*, the 1994 HBO special.

Two years into his term as president, Clinton would sign the 1994 Crime Bill with life imprisonment for three violent felonies (three strikes) and truth in sentencing with fixed terms mandated for certain crimes. State legislatures followed suit, and state penitentiary populations swelled with longer prison sentences. Additional police officers were put on the streets. Without question, the brunt of the War on Crime fell on the Black community. That affected the caseload of the appellate courts dramatically.

Moreover, the Arkansas Supreme Court when I joined in 1991 was all white, male, and old. I was the youngest member. One woman, Elsijane Trimble Roy, and two Blacks, Richard Mays and Perlesta Hollingsworth, had been appointed to serve out three justices' terms, but none had been elected. As I write this, no Black person has been elected to the Arkansas Supreme Court, although several have won elections to the Court of Appeals. Stated simply, the Supreme Court did not represent the Arkansas demographic.

***

For the first eight years, my work on the court, when coupled with my published articles on the law and Supreme Court committee work, was all consuming. It was a 24/7 job. Or at least, I made it that way. Eventually, I had an epiphany. The catalyst for my change was United States Senator Joe Lieberman, who is an orthodox Jew and in 2000 was a candidate for vice president (former Vice President Al Gore was the Democratic nominee for president). Because he was orthodox, Lieberman eschewed work on the Sabbath – Saturday. When I thought about that, I said to myself, here is a senator running for vice president of the United States, and he can refrain from work one day a week. Surely, he has more on his plate than I do. I determined to cut back, and I did.

In retrospect, I wish the epiphany and my cutback in work habits had happened earlier. In 1991, Stuart was turning fifteen and experiencing adolescence with all that entails. Peer pressure and young romance ruled the day, and that is when I knew a father is most in demand. The summer after my election, we took a float trip on the Buffalo River and camped out for a night. We swapped stories while canoeing down the river. I told him the plots of "Othello," one of Truman Capote's short stories, and really whatever came to mind.

From Pulaski Heights Junior High, we sent Stuart to Woodberry Forest School, an all-boys school in Virginia. It was always our plan that Stuart would go to boarding school. It was clearly the right decision, and he thrived there, making a host of friends and catching up academically. He was a bona fide tennis star and basketball player, which made the transition easier.

***

There was a certain ivory tower aspect to my job on the court. Two chief justices probably summed it up best. Chief Justice Bradley Jesson, who was appointed by Governor Jim Guy Tucker to serve out Chief Justice Jack Holt's term, described the work this way: "It's as if you are on an assembly line and one batch of cases comes along and you deal with those cases and are exhausted, and then another batch of cases immediately comes streaming down the line, and you start all over again. It's never ending."

Chief Justice Dub Arnold put the job this way: "It was like working in a nursing home in the Justice Building. Every now and then a justice would wander out of his room and into the hallway and it was my job to take him by the elbow and guide him back into his office." Justice John Purtle called the court a "monastery." For me, it was a kind of Purgatory where I worked for justice tirelessly, in isolation, while never being quite sure I had achieved it.

CHAPTER 19

A Legacy Review

Like most justices, my legacy on the court is best defined by the opinions and articles I wrote while there. When I was writing the farewell article on Justice George Rose Smith for the *Arkansas Lawyer* in 1986, I asked how many of his thousands of opinions he considered truly significant. We were sitting in his tree house only a few yards from his house, where he would often go to reflect.

"There were only six," he said.

I was incredulous. Here was a man who had served on the court for thirty-seven years.

"Yep, only six," he repeated, in his taciturn way. And he went on to describe them, which I listed in my article.

This led me to consider how many truly landmark opinions I had crafted. After all, I had been on the court for twenty-two years, almost three full eight-year terms, and easily had written close to eight hundred majority opinions and a considerable number of concurring opinions and dissents.

Writing opinions on major cases was heady wine for me. At times, especially early on, it seemed like I expressed my views in every case. And let me quickly add that I relied heavily on my law clerks for their comments, opinions, and memoranda. Ultimately though, it was my name on the opinion, not theirs, as the law clerks quickly pointed out to me. There was further the point that none of my majority opinions were single justice opinions. Again, majority opinions required four votes to be an opinion of the court and often ideas and wording were suggested by the other justices.

So I began my quest to decide which of my opinions were truly historic and noteworthy.

Most of my opinions did not fall into that category. For instance, early in my first year I was assigned a case where a dog escaped from the window of a car in a hospital parking lot and chased a squirrel across the lot and adjoining street before running headlong into a stopped vehicle, denting its side. *Bolstad v. Pergeson.* The dog owner had violated a city ordinance by allowing his dog to escape. That was negligence on his part, which made him liable for the property damage of $312.00. I handed down the opinion on April 1, 1991 – April Fool's Day. That was appropriate.

Somehow, this opinion did not seem as significant as education reform, same-sex issues, or death penalty cases. But it was important to the parties and involved a citizen's duty of care.

Ultimately, I arrived at a handful of cases I felt were most noteworthy, and I'll share those in the next four chapters.

CHAPTER 20

My Opinions: The System

After much prayerful consideration, I begin with major cases dealing with the elements of our system of government: the terms of our office holders, police conduct, what comprises a judge's interests, and mandatory sentencing.

Throw the Rascals Out – Term Limits

My first real ordeal by fire in a case of national significance came with *U.S. Term Limits, Inc. v. Hill,* which was assigned to me as lead justice in 1994. In November 1993, the voters in Arkansas voted overwhelmingly to amend the State Constitution with Amendment 73 to limit the terms to be served by state constitutional officers and members of the state general assembly. What was questionable was that Amendment 73 also limited the terms of United States representatives and senators from Arkansas to three terms and two terms, respectively, where the United States Constitution had no term limits. Could Arkansas curtail the terms of its federal officeholders by an amendment to its State Constitution? That was the paramount issue.

Arkansas had been no exception. Across the country, the issue of term limits for federal legislators had caught fire. The experience and power that came with longevity in Congress as well as the institutional knowledge possessed by these senior statesmen was of no great moment. The Arkansas voters wanted more control over who served in Congress in addition to state government, and their philosophy was to "throw the rascals out," if need be. The overarching constitutional question raised by this was whether Amendment 73 added another qualification to Article I of the United States Constitution in addition to age and citizenship about who could serve in Congress. If so, an amendment to that Constitution – not the State Constitution – was required with three-fourths of the states agreeing to its passage. It was not an overstatement that this decision could dramatically affect the caliber of future federal legislation.

The Term Limits case was a huge undertaking made all the more daunting by four recusals of the regular justices of my court, leaving only three regular justices to hear the case: Justice Steele Hays, Justice Bob Dudley, and me. Thus, Governor Tucker had to make four appointments of special justices, which he did: Judge Ernie Wright and Judge George Cracraft of the Court of Appeals, and Circuit Judges Carl McSpadden and Gerald Brown. They were all excellent appointments.

It was after oral argument and our first conference with the hodgepodge of regular and appointed justices that Justice Hays addressed me as "lad" and asked me if I could handle the case. My role had been to present the case to the other justices and give my recommendations, followed by each justice providing his comments. Justice Hays's consternation was no doubt due to my relative inexperience on the court but also because of the magnitude of the decision and the fact that the seven of us were split "every whicher way" on the issues. It would be a yeoman task to cobble together a majority on each point. He was right to be concerned.

I circulated my proposed majority opinion to the justices, and this was followed by several conferences and several concurring and dissenting opinions. The positions of the justices ultimately congealed this way, with all justices agreeing the case was ripe and that the lack of an enacting clause was not fatal:

Brown, Wright and McSpadden: Amendment 73 is enforceable for state officeholders, but by limiting terms of federal representatives and senators, it added another qualification to the U.S. Constitution and was unconstitutional.

Gerald Brown: Agreed Amendment 73 could not add another qualification to the U.S. Constitution. Disagreed that Amendment 73 had "severable" provisions that allowed it to amend the State Constitution.

Dudley: Concluded that Amendment 73 was completely void because severing a valid amendment to the State Constitution from an invalid amendment to the U.S. Constitution after the election was impossible since the two were inextricably linked.

Hays: Agreed that Amendment 73 was valid to amend the State Constitution. Disagreed that it could not also amend the U.S. Constitution.

Cracraft: Agreed that Amendment 73 is valid to amend State Constitution. Disagreed that Amendment 73 violated the qualification clause of the U.S. Constitution, but, rather, it was a ballot access issue. Thus, the amendment is valid for both constitutions.

With the addition of Justice Hays and Special Chief Justice Cracraft's votes on the validity of Amendment 73 to amend the State Constitution, I had five votes. With the addition of Special Justice Gerald Brown's vote to the three I had that Amendment 73 impermissibly added another qualification to the United States Constitution, I had four votes and a majority.

My recollection is that throughout this convoluted process Special Justices Wright and McSpadden were extraordinarily wise, helpful, and supportive. In retrospect, Justice Hays asked a telling question. My answer to him, of course, was "yes, I could handle it," but the solid support and advice provided by these two men made my task infinitely easier.

In striking down term limits for members of Congress, in a plurality opinion in 1995 (*U.S. Term Limits v. Hill*), I wrote:

> If there is one watchword for representation of the various states in Congress, it is uniformity. Federal legislators speak to national issues that affect the citizens of every state. Additional age restrictions,

residency requirements, or sundry experience criteria established by the states would cause variances in this uniformity and lead to an imbalance among the states with respect to who can sit in Congress. This is precisely what we believe the drafters of the U.S. Constitution intended to avoid. The uniformity in qualifications mandated in Article 1 provides the tenor and the fabric for representation in the Congress. Piecemeal restrictions by every state would fly in the face of that order.

This precise language was quoted by Justice John Paul Stevens of the United States Supreme Court when he wrote the majority opinion affirming our opinion in *U.S. Term Limits, Inc. v. Thornton* in 1995. That was a five to four decision by the United States Supreme Court, which means that if one justice had shifted on Justice Stephens, we would now have limited terms of service by our United States senators and representatives.

Knock and Talk Searches – Homeowners Must Consent to Warrantless Searches

The image of drug task force units and SWAT teams breaking down front doors without proper announcement or consent in poor neighborhoods is a vivid one and haunts the popular imagination.

It happened in the case of Breonna Taylor in Louisville, Kentucky in 2020, when the execution of a forced entry raid went awry and she was killed. Variations of no-knock raids became prevalent during the drug tumult of the 80s and 90s but became even more standard operating procedure after the Criminal Justice Act of 1994 and similar state legislation that mirrored it. Police knocking and immediately announcing who they were and then breaking down the door and searching became common practice. Consent by the homeowners was generally not required; nor was advising the homeowner of the right to refuse consent.

The Arkansas Supreme Court during the 90s was sensitive about such tactics by the police and sought to put the brakes on suspect action when it ran afoul of fundamental constitutional principles of due process and privacy. The home was sacrosanct, and without a search or arrest warrant from a judge, raids following a "knock and talk" bust into the home were given great scrutiny by the court.

This was particularly true in the minds of a majority of the Arkansas Supreme Court in 2004 when the homeowner was not told his or her right to refuse the officers' search. In *Brown v. State*, I wrote for the court:

> It is the intimidation effect of multiple police officers appearing on a home dweller's doorstep, sometimes in uniform and armed, and requesting consent to search without advising the home dweller of his or her right to refuse consent that presents the constitutional problem.

We held in *Brown* that the right to refuse such a search was part of liberty and privacy rights under the Arkansas Constitution. The Arkansas Constitution had been used in *Jegley v. Picado* (which I'll discuss in more depth in Chapter XXIII) to protect the bedroom, and now it was used to stop a warrantless search without appropriate warnings.

The *Brown* case was a narrow victory for that position – 4 to 3 to be exact – and in holding as the majority did, we deviated from federal case law and our own case of *King v. State*, which had followed federal case law and held that a warning about refusal to consent was unnecessary. The majority position, though, was not that radical. We followed case law from three other jurisdictions, New Jersey, Mississippi, and Washington, that had done the same. And in holding as we did, we followed similar precepts voiced in the *Miranda* decision against self-incrimination.

So now with the *Brown* case for home invasion protection, the Arkansas Supreme Court, using its State Constitution, had expanded privacy rights beyond what federal courts had provided under the United States Constitution. But what about pretextual searches of automobiles?

Pretextual Searches by Police Officers

In the typical pretextual case involving a car, a police officer has a "suspicion" that a felony had been committed by a driver and needs a reason to stop, arrest, and search the vehicle. The standard pretext for a stop was speeding, changing lanes, or a burned-out taillight. The stop-and-arrest was conducted, and a search for drugs incident to that arrest ensued. If drugs were found, the issue raised by the offender was suppression because of an illegal search. This could only be done under Arkansas law. Under federal law there was no longer a pretext inquiry because the subjective intent of police officers had already been deemed irrelevant by the United States Supreme Court.

The *State v. Sullivan* case in 2002 brought the pretext issue to the fore with the police officer's grounds for a stop under state law being speeding, lack of vehicle registration, no proof of insurance, and possession of a rusty hatchet. The police officer, nonetheless, had, after the stop, recognized Sullivan as one involved in narcotics in the area. He chose not to cite Sullivan for a speeding violation but to arrest him, which led to the search of the car and finding methamphetamines and drug paraphernalia. The arresting officer used the rusty hatchet as a weapon to bolster the basis for the arrest after the stop. We excluded the evidence found after the stop, and I wrote:

> Today, we solidify our position, based on the adequate and in-dependent state grounds of Article 2, section 15, of the Arkansas Constitution, as well as our own pretext decisions. Under these au-thorities, pretextual arrests – arrests that would not have occurred *but* for an ulterior investigative motive – are unreasonable police conduct warranting application of the exclusionary rule.

Thus, the Arkansas Supreme Court went beyond the federal court's interpretation of the United States Constitution by expanding protec-tions under the State Constitution and excluding evidence found by a police officer when the stop was due to a violation that was only a pretext to search the car.

This led to my article in *The Journal of Appellate Practice and Process* in the fall of 2002 describing this state expansion of fundamental rights. I pointed out how the United States Supreme Court had shown state courts how they could expand rights under their state constitutions beyond federal interpretations of the United States Constitution, and Arkansas, in particular, had successfully done so.

"You Never Stop Being a Judge." – Justice George Rose Smith

Judge Wendell Griffen has been and is a conundrum. A highly intelligent lawyer and Pulaski County circuit judge, he is also an ordained minister whose church, Emmanuel Baptist, has been a fixture in Little Rock since 1947. He is very causal and outspoken and an unrestrained activist on issues that eat away at him.

He announced plans to retire when his term expired at the end of 2022 but promised to devote "more time and energy to writing, lecturing, and discoursing about social justice and public theology." To some, it might be hard to imagine he could give such matters any more time.

Griffen once lay on a cot outside the Governor's Mansion as a protest against an imminent execution of an inmate for capital murder. A few years earlier, he lobbied the Black Caucus of legislators in the Arkansas General Assembly to engage in economic warfare against the University of Arkansas at Fayetteville as retribution for what Griffen perceived to be some of its racist practices. He had been a law student at Fayetteville and had experienced the systematic racism of the university system, he said. It mushroomed, he added, until it culminated in the firing of Nolan Richardson, the highly successful Black basketball coach of the Arkansas Razorbacks who had won a national championship. Richardson had been fired, according to the administration, because of recent lackluster success on the basketball court and some inappropriate public comments. To Griffen, Richardson's firing was blatant racism, and he said so to the Legislative Black Caucus and elsewhere.

In 2003, the Arkansas Judicial Discipline and Disability Commission called Griffen to task and sanctioned him with a public admonishment. He appealed to the Supreme Court for resolution. At issue was Canon 4C(1) of the Code of Judicial Conduct which reads:

Governmental, Civic or Charitable Activities

(1) A judge shall not appear at a public hearing before, or other-
wise consult with, an executive or legislative body or official except on
matters concerning the law, the legal system or the administration of
justice or except when acting pro se in a matter involving the judge or
the judge's interests.

What were the judge's "interests?" Did that refer only to financial
interests, as the dissenters believed, or was the term much broader,
embracing personal beliefs of the judge as well?

We reversed the Commission's sanction. My point in writing the
majority opinion in a 4 to 3 decision in *Griffen v. Arkansas Judicial
Discipline and Disability Commission* was we did not know. The term
"interests" was vague and undefined. I wrote:

> Without a standard established in the "judge's interests" exception
> to Canon 4C(1) to guide Judge Griffen on what is a proper area of
> comment to the legislative officials, we are hard-pressed to find a vio-
> lation of the canon. And without proof of a "narrow tailoring" of the
> exception by the Judicial Commission when the parameters of speech
> based on conduct are directly involved, Canon 4C(1), as applied to
> Judge Griffen, violates his First Amendment rights.

Dissenter Justice Don Corbin argued that it was ludicrous for the
court not to know what it meant by "interests," because the court had
adopted the canon at issue. That was easily answered because the issue
was not what the court knew or intended but what Griffen thought the
parameters of the term were based on the rule's plain language.

As far as judicial free speech, the United States Supreme Court, a
year earlier in *Republican Party of Minnesota v. White*, had held that
any limitation on a judge announcing his views must be "narrowly
tailored" to serve a compelling state interest. We held in *Griffen* that the
Judicial Commission had not met that standard and, thus, had violated
Griffen's free speech rights as well.

The court's decision in favor of Griffen's judicial speech rights was not a popular one in some quarters. An editorial in the *Arkansas Democrat-Gazette* called my opinion a disgrace. Later, I saw Judge Griffen at a public gathering. He sidled up to me and stuck out his hand. "Thank you," he said.

One Strike and You're Out

A dissent can carry the day, either by changing the minds of the court's majority or by persuading another court on review. I am often asked what I look for in a case or focus on in oral arguments. The answer is always what is just and legal. But ultimately it is "What is fair?" And that is where dissents come in.

There was one case, *Henderson v. State*, in 1995, where the defendant got life imprisonment for the sale of three rocks of crack cocaine – less than a quarter of a gram – worth $20. The state statute permitted this. It was Grover Henderson's first offense. The image of Jean Valjean being sentenced to five years in prison for stealing one loaf of bread in Victor Hugo's *Les Miserables* immediately came to mind.

On appeal, four justices on my court affirmed the conviction and sentence, but three justices dissented. I wrote for the dissenters, and the case finally went to the Eighth Circuit Court of Appeals on a petition for a writ of habeas corpus, questioning why the defendant was imprisoned. The Eighth Circuit granted the writ, thus vacating the sentence, and released Henderson on grounds that the sentence was grossly unfair and violated the Eighth Amendment's prohibition against "cruel and unusual punishment."

Judge Morris Arnold of Arkansas wrote the opinion for the Eighth Circuit granting the writ and Henderson's release. He said:

> We first note that, with respect to Mr. Henderson's direct appeal to the Arkansas Supreme Court, the dissent, in which three of the seven judges joined, states that "[t]his is the first time that a life sentence has been affirmed in this State where the defendant's crime was one offense and a first offense and where the quantity of drugs sold was such a minor amount," *Henderson*, 322 Ark. at 413, 910

S.W.2d at 661 (Brown, J., dissenting). The dissent went on to list other Arkansas decisions in which life sentences were affirmed, *see id.*, 322 Ark. at 414-15, 910 S.W.2d at 662, but all of them involved repeat offenders or more serious crimes. The dissent concluded that the sentence was so wholly disproportionate to the nature of the offense as to shock the moral sense of the community," *id.*, 322 Ark. at 413, 910 S.W.2d at 661.

Later, in visiting with Judge Arnold, he ranked his opinion in *Henderson* as among the most important opinions he had written. Today, when we question the efficiency and fairness of our criminal justice system from top to bottom, the *Henderson* case stands out as a beacon for justice.

CHAPTER 21

My Opinions: The Business World

Fair and open competition is a cornerstone of our system of capitalism. This was the issue in the Wal-Mart case in 1995, when the question was whether Wal-Mart (which now goes by Walmart) was engaging in predatory practices against a mom-and-pop store in Conway, Arkansas, when it dropped prices. Wal-Mart's business model had been called into question, and the future of the retailer was at a critical juncture.

"Court Backs Wal-Mart on Pricing," *The New York Times,* January 10, 1995

Discount stores were proliferating in the 1980s. Gibson's in Little Rock comes to mind but also K-Mart on a much grander scale. But no one was prepared for the behemoth that soon took center stage – Wal-Mart. Out of nowhere, Sam Walton from Newport, a five and dime store manager, conceived and implemented a retail sales model that transformed the industry.

We in Arkansas know the story. Walton was savvy enough to stock the items consumers wanted and were buying. He would stock and restock and track goods by telephone calls and then by computer to determine what was selling and what was needed. It was revolutionary. He bought in bulk and kept close tabs on what was coming in and going out. And if need be, he would have sales and reduce popular items to below market cost to bring buyers into his stores. That was the loss leader strategy employed by many retailers to attract customers.

But Wal-Mart became so successful that small businesses like pharmacies in Conway began to complain about its practices. Eventually, they complained Wal-Mart was engaged in predatory pricing – an unfair trade practice – that was throttling competition by selling products below cost. During this time, Wal-Mart's strategy was to locate on the outskirts of a town just off a major highway or interstate and draw its buyers from the surrounding areas. Meanwhile, mom and pop stores in the business center of towns like Conway began to feel the competitive impact.

Eventually, several pharmacy outlets in Conway filed suit alleging that Wal-Mart was violating the Arkansas Unfair Trade Practices Act. The trial court in Conway agreed and assessed treble damages to punish Wal-Mart. The court inferred a purpose by Wal-Mart to destroy competition by using the loss leader strategy. Wal-Mart appealed.

In a four-to-three decision in 1995, my court reversed the trial court in *Wal-Mart Stores, Inc. v. American Drugs, Inc.* The three special justices appointed by Governor Jim Guy Tucker to sit on the case dissented on the basis that Wal-Mart's aggressive competitive strategies, including using loss leaders, injured and destroyed competition. The four regular justices, including me, formed the majority.

Writing for the majority, I said:

> In the case before us, the loss-leader strategy employed by Conway Wal-Mart is readily justifiable as a tool to foster competition and to gain a competitive edge as opposed to simply being viewed as a stratagem to eliminate rivals altogether. We are further sensitive to the ultimate purpose of the Arkansas Unfair Practices Act to foster competition and to protect the public against the destruction of competition and the creation and perpetuation of monopolies. Certainly legitimate competition in the marketplace can, and often does, result in economic injury to competitors. A competitor that has been injured by legitimate competitive pricing, though, should not

be permitted to use the Arkansas Act as a fountain for recouping its losses. In short, the circumstances of this case are not sufficiently egregious to prove that Conway Wal-Mart crossed the line with regard to predatory prices and purposeful destruction of competition.

Stated differently, we held that just showing that Wal-Mart used below costs sales was not enough to prove an intent to drive competitors out of business. Indeed, the proof showed that the suing pharmacies were still making a profit despite competition from Wal-Mart. Just not as much.

So Wal-Mart survived and lived to compete another day with a loss leader option available to it. And compete it did, dominating retail until a new seller with revolutionary strategies began to assert itself: Amazon – with online buying and two-day delivery.

Prior Restraint on the Press

In 2000, Juvenile Judge Stacey Zimmerman enjoined the press from naming or photographing a juvenile defendant, twelve-year-old Michael Nichols, who had shot and wounded a police officer and was now appearing in her court. Nichols was then photographed leaving the courthouse by an *Arkansas Democrat-Gazette* photographer. Judge Zimmerman cited the newspaper for contempt of court for violating her order and fined it $100. The newspaper immediately asked for emergency relief from the Arkansas Supreme Court to modify Judge Zimmerman's order on grounds that it constituted a prior restraint on the press.

The Supreme Court agreed in *Arkansas Democrat-Gazette v. Zimmerman*. I wrote the opinion for the Court, supporting the press and said:

> We . . . hold that the gag order was too pervasive in its scope. Surely the juvenile judge must protect participants in her proceedings from harassment and maintain the dignity of her court. But once the juvenile proceedings have been open to the public, we discern no overriding state interest that would warrant an injunction

against photographing Nichols and the others entering or leaving the Courthouse.

I was later advised that the *Democrat-Gazette* won a journalism award for bringing the lawsuit and succeeding. An editor of the paper later commented to the press association that he was certainly pleased with the result but viewed how the opinion was written with less enthusiasm. Oh, well, the result was what mattered.

CHAPTER 22

My Opinions: Cultural Shifts

I once was interviewed about whether cultural shifts in society's thinking influenced judicial opinions. My answer was not overtly, but as former United States Supreme Court Justice William Douglas once said, "We all read the newspapers."

The Arkansas Supreme Court has been on the cutting edge of protecting privacy rights for same sex couples. I give two examples. The first is when the court struck down the state's sodomy law. The second opinion ruled unconstitutional an initiated act forbidding unmarried adults from fostering or adopting children.

A second series of opinions I authored concerning education are probably the most significant I wrote on the court. They concerned whether an equal and adequate education was being provided to public school students, as our Arkansas Constitution requires. The Lake View cases changed the landscape for public education in Arkansas.

Prohibiting the Sword of Damocles for Gays and Lesbians

But first, there is the constitutional right to privacy in one's bedroom. The legal maxim that your home is your castle is universally revered and has been sacrosanct under Arkansas common law for more than a hundred and fifty years. Running counter to this maxim was a deep-seated bias against gay and lesbian couples that had generations of support in Arkansas. In some cases, this bias had been fostered in churches. In other instances, it was fostered by an aversion to people who adhered to a different morality. Whatever the reason, the prejudice was real and pronounced and often dangerous.

In recent years, there had been a thawing in this rigidness. There were many reasons for the cultural shift. More contact with openly homosexual couples generated a better understanding. Plus, the fact that more teenagers and young adults were "coming out of the closet" and were vocal about their sexuality spawned a reassessment in attitudes on the part of many. If your son or daughter fell into that category, you would hardly take up a cudgel against similarly positioned young adults.

One of the pivotal cases by the Arkansas Supreme Court announced protection for couples, opposite sex or same sex, who practiced non-commercial sodomy by consent in private. The case, *Jegley v. Picado*, written by Justice Annabelle Tuck in 2002, struck down an Arkansas statute criminalizing the act of sodomy on privacy and equality grounds. In doing so, the Arkansas Supreme Court relied on those rights protected in the Arkansas Constitution and not on protections in the United States Constitution.

The *Jegley* decision got a jump on what the United States Supreme Court would do the following year in the case of *Lawrence v. Texas*. In *Lawrence*, the Court held sodomy statutes in thirteen states invalid under the liberty and privacy rights protected under the Due Process Clause of the United States Constitution. The Court cited the *Jegley* case as partial authority for its decision.

I wrote a concurring opinion in *Jegley* where I challenged the State's argument that gays and lesbians who had not been charged under the sodomy statute had no grounds to contest its validity. Not so, I wrote. Even without a formal arrest, the potential for an arrest for practicing sodomy hung over their heads like a Sword of Damocles that could fall at any moment. I went on to emphasize the changing mores in the country:

Thirty years ago I daresay most religious denominations would have supported the existence of the sodomy statutes or something akin to it. Today, five religious denominations have filed an *amicus* brief in this case challenging the sodomy statute's constitutionality. The unmistakable trend, both nationally and in Arkansas, is to curb government intrusions at the threshold of one's door and most definitely at the threshold of one's bedroom.

Four years after *Jegley,* the Arkansas Supreme Court voided a regulation of its Department of Human Services which prevented gays and lesbians from being foster parents. That was in the *Howard* case written by Justice Don Corbin. According to the testimony of DHS witnesses before the trial court, homosexuality was a sin and immoral and homosexual parenting would endanger the health of foster children. Countering this testimony was the fact that no evidence or data supported this conclusion concerning danger. We noted in *Howard* that any public policy decision excluding homosexuals was for the General Assembly to legislate and not for an executive branch agency like DHS to adopt on its own. I agreed with that reasoning but concurred because I further believed the DHS Regulation excluding homosexuals violated equality and privacy rights of those excluded individuals under the Arkansas Constitution.

As a direct result of our *Howard* decision, the General Assembly enacted Initiated Act 1 in 2001, which prohibited anyone from fostering or adopting children if that person lived with another person outside of marriage. Act 1 applied to opposite sex and same sex couples. It clearly was aimed at thwarting homosexuals from fostering and adopting.

* * *

Ten years later in 2011, I wrote a unanimous opinion for the court where we took another major step in expanding the rights of same sex couples. The case was *Arkansas Department of Human Services v. Cole.* In *Cole*, the Court tackled the issue of whether gay and lesbian couples would be permitted to foster and adopt children, which was foreclosed by Act 1, since the couples were not married.

In striking down Initiated Act 1, I wrote that individual assessments of potential gay and lesbian couples as adoptive or foster parents by the government were ample protection against unfit foster or adoptive parents:

> We conclude that the individualized assessments by DHS and our trial courts are effective in addressing issues such as relationship instability, abuse, lack of social support, and other factors that could potentially create a risk to the child or otherwise render the applicant unsuitable to be a foster or adoptive parent. These would be the least restrictive means for addressing the compelling state interest of protecting the welfare, safety, and best interest of Arkansas's children. By imposing a categorical ban on all persons who cohabit with a sexual partner, Act 1 removes the ability of the State and our courts to conduct these individualized assessments on these individuals, many of whom could qualify and be entirely suitable foster or adoptive parents.

I was convinced, as was a unanimous court, that an absolute ban on unmarried couple adoptions was shortsighted, especially since no proof was offered that this would be harmful to prospective foster and adopted children. The *Cole* opinion opened the door to a whole host of qualified same sex couples who could now appropriately foster and adopt children. In the process, a critical need was met and multiple children entered into a stable and loving environment.

Adequate and Equal Public Education – The *Lake View* Saga

I am convinced that no opinion that I wrote was as important to the future of Arkansas as the Lake View opinion. Actually, there were six Lake View opinions that I authored.

The Arkansas Constitution, in Article 14, Section 1, says that, "The State shall ever maintain a general suitable and sufficient system of free public schools and shall adopt all suitable means to secure to the people the advantage and opportunities of education."

"Suitable" public education in Arkansas has always been tied to better roads to transport children to school, sufficient funds for education through property taxes, and parental commitment to education for their children. For years a barometer of how well a school district was doing in meeting its constitutional mandate was its per pupil expenditures. Wealthier school districts could provide more funds based on property taxes to their students, and a disparity in educational opportunity compared to poorer school districts was the result.

This problem of disparate funding followed by disparate educational opportunity was not solely an Arkansas problem. As then-Governor Bill Clinton put it in 1983 after he read the book *A Nation at Risk: The Imperative for Educational Reform,* in which an appointed education commission described the country's failing education system: "If the nation as a whole is failing in education, Arkansas's system must be on life support."

That same year, the Arkansas Supreme Court held in the case of *Dupree v. Alma School District* that the Arkansas school system discriminated against its children, from school district to school district, on the basis of wealth and thus was unconstitutional under the Arkansas Constitution.

Having just rewon the governorship in 1982 from Frank White, Clinton needed a bold issue to make his mark. Education filled that need. He commissioned his wife Hillary to do a comprehensive seventy-five county assessment of the state of education in Arkansas. She reported back in the late summer of 1983 that Arkansas needed to raise its educational standards dramatically, which included instituting mandatory kindergartens, reduced class size, a longer school year, and a program for gifted and talented children. She also recommended that all teachers be tested for basic skills in literacy, math, and science. The Arkansas Teachers Union howled in dismay.

In October 1983, Clinton called a special session of the General Assembly to tackle the proposed reforms and teacher testing and to pass a 1 percent increase in the sales tax to equalize educational opportunity. The Arkansas General Assembly jumped into high gear and passed the sales tax increase to equalize expenditures among school districts and to fund the education reforms, including teacher testing. The teacher testing issue was to catapult Clinton into national prominence.

Much more was to come. In 1992, the rural Lake View School District (Phillips County) brought a suit claiming the state's funding system for public education violated the state and United States constitutions. Chancery Judge Annabelle Imber (now Tuck) ruled in 1994 that the education system not only still discriminated on the basis of wealth but was inadequate, which meant school children were not learning basic math, reading, and writing skills so as to function in today's world.

The response was Constitutional Amendment 74, which was adopted by the people of Arkansas in 1996 and required that a uniform property tax of 25 mills be assessed in all school districts for the maintenance and operation of the schools. Unsatisfied, the Lake View district filed amended complaints arguing that the remedies were insufficient.

Judge Tuck was then elected to the Arkansas Supreme Court and the *Lake View* case, as it was known, was assigned to Chancery Judge Collins Kilgore, who first ruled that any constitutional challenge was moot in light of Amendment 74 and the additional funding it generated. We on the Supreme Court disagreed and sent the matter back to Judge Kilgore to determine whether there had been compliance with Judge Tuck's 1994 order, notwithstanding the adoption of Amendment 74. Judge Kilgore held comprehensive hearings and ruled that school districts were unequally funded and that the education provided was inadequate and, thus, not suitable under the Arkansas Constitution.

Kilgore's order was appealed to the Arkansas Supreme Court, which determined that the matter of assuring a suitable public education was solely in the hands of the state and not the individual school districts and their superintendents. Carol Dalby from Texarkana was appointed by Governor Mike Huckabee to replace Justice Tuck, who had recused. Writing for the court in a forty-page opinion, I made it clear that the State Department of Education must assure the money is benefiting individual students equally and not merely distributed equally to the state's school districts. I further agreed with Judge Kilgore that the percentage of high school graduates entering college who needed additional education in the basics, which they should have learned in high school, was impermissibly high. Hence, I agreed with Judge Tuck and Judge Kilgore that our system of public education in Arkansas was failing and inadequate. We held that "the State has an absolute duty under our Constitution to provide an adequate education to each school child."

The *Lake View* opinion was handed down in November 2002. The opinion further required that education be funded first at each regular legislative session and that an adequacy hearing be held before each session to hear experts on whether Arkansas was complying.

In January 2003, Governor Mike Huckabee made his State of the State address to the General Assembly. The smart money was on Huckabee doing the least he could do to increase funding for public education, but he surprised us all. He urged a full overhaul of state education and not a mere Band-Aid solution. He even went beyond our decision and advocated for a consolidation of school districts to provide better efficiency and course opportunities for more students. His plan was to reduce the state's 310 school districts to 130.

Thus began the saga of the *Lake View* case that rumbled on for another seven years with me writing at least six opinions. Lake View attorney Bill Llewellyn used the metaphor at one early oral argument that the Arkansas Supreme Court was like Jacob wrestling with God. "Once you grab ahold, you can't let go." He was urging the court not to release jurisdiction of the case. My response to lawyer Llewellyn was that we all know what happened to Jacob in the Bible story. He was struck lame by God. A friend who was sitting next to Governor Huckabee in the courtroom said the governor almost fell out of his chair, he was laughing so hard.

Masters were later appointed (former Chief Justice Brad Jesson and retired Justice David Newbern) to make findings of fact about compliance, and mandates signifying compliance were issued by the court and then recalled when compliance fell short. Facilities, equipment, and teachers' pay were reviewed, and deficiencies were highlighted by the masters and then by my court. All this required more state funds. Following the last masters' report, the court ruled the public school system was constitutional in 2007. I wrote:

> What is especially meaningful to this Court is the Masters' finding that the General Assembly has expressly shown that constitutional compliance in the field of education is an ongoing task requiring constant study, review, and adjustment. In the Court's view, Act 57 . . . requiring annual legislative review by legislative committees, and Act 108 . . . establishing education as the State's funding priority, are the cornerstones for assuring future compliance.

The *Lake View* decisions provided that, under state administration, considerably more state money would be funneled into the public schools for facilities, teacher salaries, and equalizing state aid among the school districts. Some chafed at the idea of just throwing money at the education "problem." In conversations with *Arkansas Democrat-Gazette* publisher Walter Hussman, he was convinced that good education was the direct result of good teachers. Everything else was secondary. My retort was always that decent facilities, equipment, and accessories were integral to good teacher performance. If a teacher in Lake View taught in outdated classrooms with outdated equipment and a leaking ceiling, he or she began with a marked disadvantage.

Debates over the efficacy of *Lake View* dollars still rage on. Governors Huckabee, Beebe, and Hutchinson generally supported the cornerstone principles of equality and adequacy embedded in *Lake View*, but the General Assembly still arches its back at times over the financial burden of what the Supreme Court mandated. And yet, no one can deny the strides made in education during the *Lake View* years and beyond. Mike Huckabee's Director of Education, Ray Simon, summarized the Arkansas progress with excitement and pride in 2008. "Buddy, I tell you. Arkansas is a player now." Indeed, Arkansas has become a model and blueprint on how best to overhaul an antiquated, unequal, and inadequate system of state education.

CHAPTER 23

My Opinions: The Ultimate Penalty

Death penalty cases were the most difficult for me and, I daresay, for most members of the court. Before my election, I had told people like Senator Dale Bumpers that I had reservations about the death penalty on moral, religious, and decency grounds. But when I decided to run for the court, I reassessed my position as an absolute opponent of the death penalty and determined that I would review death cases on the merits, which meant I would study the facts, especially the aggravating and mitigating circumstances as the statutes required, and the law, and then make my decision.

That is not to say I would review death cases cavalierly. On the contrary, with death as the penalty, I always felt the terrible burden of these decisions and gave them my full attention.

My good friend, Judge Richard Arnold, told me that on occasion he would consult with a spiritual adviser when making a decision in a death case. That was not my practice, but my thought was that a judge in a death case should follow any guidance or ritual that makes that judge comfortable, including spiritual consultation. I will say I was always aware when the person's execution took place when I had affirmed his or her death sentence.

If the truth be known, most of the justices I served with were far removed from the harsh reality of a death sentence. Chief Justice Dub Arnold was the exception. As a prosecutor and then circuit judge, he had attended several executions, including ones by lethal injection and one by electrocution. But for the rest of us, an execution was more of an abstract event that was read about but not experienced up close and personal.

When I became a deputy prosecuting attorney in 1970, I did make a trip down to Cummins penitentiary because I wanted to see where those I convicted would serve their time. It was on that trip when the prison guards closed the doors on me because I was dressed all in khaki – the uniform of a prison trusty. The lowest ranking prisoners were the rankmen, who dressed all in white. The next category were the DoPops, who dressed in white pants and khaki shirts. Then the trusties. Before Governor Winthrop Rockefeller's administration, trusties ran the prison. The trip to Cummins was an education and would not be my last. But when I became a Supreme Court justice, I did not have the same motivation to witness an execution. Knowing that death was the end result was all I needed to know.

Before I assumed the bench in 1991, Alan Leverett, the publisher of the *Arkansas Times* magazine, called me for lunch. We were friends, and the invitation was not unusual. During our meal, Alan asked me if I was going to vote against the death penalty on the court and urged me to do so. My answer was swift and simple: "How could I keep faith with the Arkansas people if I prejudged all death sentences?" If I were disposed to do that, I added, I should have told the voters during the campaign that I was irrevocably opposed to the death penalty and would vote accordingly. To his credit, he understood my reasoning and never mentioned it again.

There was one justice on the court whom I served with who, I suspected, did have reservations about the death penalty and never voted for it while we served together. And yet, he seemed to always vote to affirm criminal convictions and sentences where the penalty was less than death. It was an interesting approach to criminal sentencing, and I am certain that justice rationalized what he did in his own mind.

So if the facts and the law warranted it, I would vote to affirm death sentences, and I wrote a few opinions upholding a death sentence. I will say I was always aware when the person's execution took place when I had affirmed his or her death sentence. Moments of silence and a prayer seemed always appropriate.

For example, on July 14, 2020, there was a federal execution of Daniel Lewis Lee for murdering a three-member Arkansas family. I had voted to affirm Lee's death sentence in 1994 in his direct appeal to the Arkansas Supreme Court.

On occasion, there were cases where the vote to affirm a death sentence was 4 to 3. Some of those executions were carried out. Typically, when the vote for a death sentence was 4 to 3, Justice Don Corbin would proclaim, "How can we affirm death when the split on the court shows three of us have considerable doubt about guilt or the sentence?" It was a valid point but usually did not carry the day. On one occasion we had to track down a justice who was out of state to have four votes affirm a death sentence.

Howard v. State in 2002 was just such a situation that Justice Corbin abhorred. A man and woman had been murdered, and there had been an attempted murder of their child. The court affirmed a death sentence with three justices dissenting, myself included. Justice Corbin had recused on the case. The evidence against Howard was weak and circumstantial. As much as anything, the murders suggested a drug deal gone bad. Part of the prosecution's case was two cowboy boots found in a field standing side-by-side with Howard's blood on one boot. Another piece of evidence was a Mountain Dew bottle with Howard's fingerprint on it.

After my court's affirmance, the case went to federal court and a new trial was granted. On retrial, Howard was convicted of second-degree murder and sentenced to serve thirty-eight years. We affirmed on appeal, and Howard was released soon after that for time served. So punishment went from a death sentence to release under a sentence for a lesser offense. The criminal justice system eventually got it right, but after years of floundering. Following the first appeal to the Arkansas Supreme Court, Howard was to be executed after a four-to-three decision. Only the federal court's intervention prevented that from happening.

Two cases where the courts did not get it right until it was too late were Charles Laverne Singleton and Ricky Ray Rector.

Singleton had been sentenced to death in the 1980s, but because of his schizophrenia, he was not sufficiently aware to know he was about to be put to death without taking his anti-psychotic medication to center him. Stated differently, his medication made him sufficiently sane to be executed.

Singleton's guilt had been determined through the appeal process, as had the propriety of the death sentence. In 2004, only a gubernatorial pardon could save him. Then-Attorney General Mike Beebe advised Governor Mike Huckabee that Singleton was out of appeals. A pardon was denied, and he was executed in January 2004.

Rector's similar case had occurred earlier and had drawn much media attention. Rector had unquestionably shot and killed two people, including a police officer. He then shot himself in the head and suffered a frontal lobotomy that did not kill him. The same question arose as with Singleton: did Rector know what was about to happen to him with the execution, which was the test for mental competency?

Bill Clinton was running for president at the time but was still governor of Arkansas and possessed the pardoning power. He refused to pardon Rector, and Rector was executed in January 1992. The execution caused a major stir. Was clemency denied because Clinton was running for president and wanted to appear tough on crime? There was certainly that accusation. During his execution, Rector moaned in pain as nurses tried to find usable veins for the injections.

Later, in February 2002, in the case of *Atkins v. Virginia*, the United States Supreme Court ruled execution of the mentally retarded to be cruel and unusual punishment under the 8th Amendment. Would that reasoning extend to Singleton and his schizophrenia or to Rector, who suffered from a self-imposed frontal lobotomy? Obviously no, according to jurists and governors at the time. Today, proceeding with those executions is more in doubt as the *Atkins* reasoning has been expanded to apply to a broader array of cases.

* * *

Late in my tenure on the court, the three-drug cocktail for executions was under much scrutiny, not only in Arkansas but across the country. The core issue was whether the convicted murderer felt pain during the execution. The three drugs that made up the cocktail were, first, midazolam, which was a sedative to put the offender to sleep. Then came the paralytic, vecuronium, which stopped the breathing. Last, there was the coup de gras, potassium chloride, to stop the heart.

In these cases, the state attorney general would argue that the law did not require executions to be completely painless but only that they not be cruel and unusual punishment. Advocates for the death offenders contended that the cocktail violated the 8th Amendment's cruel and unusual protection by causing what amounted to considerable pain.

Several other problems were associated with these executions. Physicians did not ordinarily participate in carrying out executions because of their Hippocratic Oaths. The question then arose whether, under the legislature's Method of Execution Act, personnel at the Department of Correction alone should be deciding the drugs injected and how to administer the drugs as part of execution by legal injection? Or did this amount to too much of a delegation of power to DOC functionaries to make policy decisions?

My court decided in 2012 (*Hobbs v. Jones*) that it was an impermissible delegation of authority by the legislature to the Department of Correction in 2012. The Method of Execution Act at issue gave the DOC no direction in deciding the chemicals to be used and the administration, and, therefore, abdicated its responsibility. I agreed with the majority and was of a mind that it was incumbent on the General Assembly to spell out in precise detail the drugs to be used in the cocktails, the dosages, and the procedures for administration. But that view did not carry the day.

CHAPTER 24

A Few Indelible
Impressions of the Court

In addition to the major cases and opinions that defined my tenure, I have also now had time to reflect on several other indelible impressions from my time on the court – how we operated, some of the notable visitors to our court, a case that dogged me, the creation of a vital program for attorneys, and the importance of a court that's accessible to the public's view. These, too, are worth remembering.

The Court as a Team

How did the court function on a personal level during my time with six other strong personalities? There was some congeniality – joint lunches and the like. There were practical jokes like Justice Paul Danielson's putting yellow crime scene tape around Justice Corbin's car in the garage and Justice Corbin lowering my chair in the conference room until my chin almost touched the table. But at times it was a court riven by rivalries and suspicion. There were always cliques and like personalities drawn to one another, all of which I chalked up to human nature.

Similar judicial philosophies led to a practice that was pernicious – the pre-conferencing or post-conferencing of cases outside the formal conferences. This amounted to lobbying for a point of view, which is fine but should not be done in the shadows. Unbeknownst to a justice not part of the pre-conferencing, he or she could walk into the formal conference where the deck has been stacked and the case for all intents and purposes has been decided before or after the conference.

Some justices like Justice Annabelle Imber Tuck viewed the practice as so abhorrent that she forbade her law clerks to talk to other law clerks about particular cases. She wanted it only to be hammered out in conference. Her position did not endear her to other justices, but she was adamant about her stance. She was right.

More serious were the leaks of court decisions to friends or the press outside of regular channels. Nothing undercut confidence in the judiciary more than this favoritism meted out by certain justices. Yet, it did go on, which I knew about even before I became a member of the court. A justice would alert a friend he previously had worked with about a pending decision, or an overly exuberant justice would blurt out a result with friends on the golf course or at a party before it was made public. That happened. But I hasten to add, not very often.

To assume the justices were not political animals would be naïve in the extreme. And we all read the newspapers, as Justice Douglas pointed out. That's not to say we were unduly influenced by public opinion, but we certainly knew what was going on. Our independence from majority views while I was on the court is best illustrated by the opinions I have already highlighted on term limits, education, the death penalty, and rights of same sex couples. All these decisions at the time ran counter to public sentiment.

My colleagues and I decided cases based on the law and our sense of what was right. Rarely in my time of service did I suspect a justice had changed a vote based on political influence. In fact, my court rated very high in its independence from partisan pressures. A study done of the state supreme courts between 1998 and 2000 entitled "Which States have The Best (and Worst) High Courts?" ranked the Arkansas Supreme Court as the second best of all the courts. Law professors from the University of Chicago, New York University, and Duke University conducted the study. Three criteria were used: productivity of the justices in issuing opinions (how quickly and how many), independence from partisan pressures, and citation of opinions by other courts. The study was released in 2008. High praise.

There are certainly weapons available to the justices to make a point publicly or to attack a colleague. The press is the most formidable weapon. Leaked information about what happened to a case in conference was verboten. And yet it happens, which, again, undermines public confidence, which is so critically important to the integrity and respect of all courts.

Supreme Visitors

On April 5, 1996, Dean Leonard Strickman of the University of Arkansas School of Law had a unique moot court competition in Fayetteville. The three-judge court was comprised of Justice Ruth Bader Ginsburg, Judge Richard Sheppard Arnold, and his brother, Judge Morris Arnold. Charlotte and I were late for the competition, but the next morning we joined Justice Ginsberg, her husband Marty, and the Strickmans (Leonard and Danielle) for breakfast. It was a memorable experience then but even more so now upon recollection.

The Ginsburgs played true to type. The ebullient Marty held forth, not in an offensive way, and charmed us all about music (he loved Gilbert and Sullivan and more traditional opera). The justice rarely said a word.

She and I compared notes about Columbia University, where we had both earned degrees. I further mentioned the fact that our term limits case for United States representatives and senators was on its way to her court. She did not miss a beat. "You sent us a good one," she said. As it happened, the decision was handed down by her court the following month, and she was with the majority affirming my decision.

Other visitors to our court conference room included Justice Antonin Scalia, Justice Stephen Breyer, and Justice Clarence Thomas. They, too, were high points. All three were extremely sociable, and Justice Scalia was candid to a fault. He admitted that at Harvard Law School he was second to Judge Richard Arnold academically. They were, in fact, good friends. After Richard's death, Justice Scalia was the first Richard S. Arnold speaker at the UALR Law School.

The West Memphis Three

One case of international focus, known as the "West Memphis Three," dogged me throughout my time on the court. Three teenage boys, Damien Echols (age eighteen), Jason Baldwin (age sixteen), and Jessie Misskelley (age seventeen), had been charged and convicted of murdering three young boys outside of West Memphis as part of a satanic ritual. Echols had gotten the death penalty. The other two got life in prison. Misskelley testified against his cohorts and described the murders.

My court affirmed the convictions in 1994 with Justice Dudley writing a ninety-page opinion for the court. Following that, the case made its way through the federal system and then new evidence compelled further review by my court. In the fall of 2010, oral arguments were held. On the first day, the oral arguments were live-streamed for all the world to see. Chief Justice Jim Hannah and I had long championed live videos of our oral arguments, and on this day it became a reality.

Following the oral arguments, the court granted the West Memphis Three a new trial. Surprisingly, the following year the three entered Alford pleas, which allowed them to plead guilty to lesser charges while still asserting their innocence. They were released for time served (over eighteen years). I was driving to North Carolina with Charlotte when I heard the news on the radio. An Alford plea was baffling to me and inconsistent on its face.

Books have been written about the murders (*The Devil's Knot* by Mara Leveritt*)* and three HBO documentaries entitled *Paradise Lost* have been made. In the third *Paradise Lost* the court was depicted in session, including myself.

My question, as in the Sandbar Rape Case, remains: Was justice served? My conclusion is the full story of the West Memphis Three has yet to be told.

Addiction and Recovery – A Safe Haven for Lawyers and Judges

In 1992, I wrote *In re Crossley*, which analyzed the issue of moral character and fitness of aspirants to practice law in Arkansas. It was also one of the first opinions, if not the first, where the Arkansas Supreme

Court recognized alcohol and drug addiction as diseases and not as voluntary conditions.

In *Crossley*, the applicant for admission to practice law admitted he suffered from the disease of chemical dependency. He had graduated from law school and passed the bar examination. He had been sober for two years, but before that he relapsed twice: once with wine and once with the illegal use of cocaine. Was he now fit to practice law as the Arkansas Rules Governing Admission to Practice Law required? The Board of Law Examiners said no, and the case was appealed to our court.

At the time, the Arkansas Supreme Court was one of the few courts, if not the only court, that did not have a program to identify impaired law students, attorneys, and judges, so as to put them on the road to recovery.

In discussing the *Crossley* case in the conference following oral argument and afterward, Chief Justice Jack Holt was vocal and passionate about the court needing to do more to police Arkansas attorneys for chemical abuse problems, which often were associated with depression. Bad acts by the affected lawyers often followed.

It soon came to light that the Arkansas Bar Association had a committee investigating just that – problems in the profession with acts of legal malpractice directly related to alcohol and substance abuse. Research was then done by Chris Thomas, director of the court's Office of Special Programs. He confirmed to me that Arkansas was almost alone in not having a program dealing with the alcohol and substance abuse issue for its lawyers and judges. Chris and I looked at one another and said: "The time is now."

This led to the creation of JLAP (Judges and Lawyers Assistance Program) in Arkansas, funded by a percentage of Bar Association dues paid by the membership. The actual creation of JLAP was a matter of Chris Thomas and me taking the Tennessee *per curiam* creating its program and changing the name to Arkansas. Later, law students were accepted into the program for substance abuse issues.

There was some objection at first by a couple of justices who termed it just another "do good" program, suggesting it did not have much merit to it. But those justices were quickly won over by the program's excellent directors, Gail Harbour and then Sarah Cearley. Added to this was the fact that while the court was considering JLAP, a well-known and well-liked judge in Conway committed suicide. The rumors were rife that he was severely depressed. No doubt the demands of his court added to that burden. What better proof was there of the dire need for an assistance program in Arkansas for a judges and lawyers?

JLAP flourishes today and is a vibrant part of the court's role in fostering an efficient, healthy, and morally attuned legal profession. I was told early in my pursuit of a JLAP program that researchers estimate 20 percent of medical and law students suffer from potential substance abuse and addiction problems. If it is only one-half of that, it is a catastrophic problem that deserves our full attention. I am as proud of the JLAP program as any achievement I had on the court. The Justice Robert L. Brown Award is given each year at the JLAP fundraiser to someone who has furthered the JLAP cause.

Demystifying the Court

The virtues of campaigning for a seat on the Supreme Court have already been underscored, but they bear repeating. What you learn about the state and its people in political campaigns pays huge dividends, and it is just plain fun. At fairs, auction barns, parades, and courthouses, you learn a lesson about human nature. Ninety-nine percent of the people you meet are welcoming and interested.

After election, it is still important to get out among the folks and demystify the court as much as possible. My serious mistake after I was elected was being too sensitive about socializing with my lawyer friends and supporters who had vigorous law practices and might have cases before the Supreme Court at any time. I erred too much on the side of being detached.

Live streaming of oral arguments with the justices, which began in 2010, has been a decided plus in opening up the court. The public as well as students can see exactly how the court operates. My only regret is that the United States Supreme Court will not follow suit in live streaming their oral arguments. I have written about this and stated my views. Not doing so is a real disservice to the people of this country.

Equally as important is Justice on Wheels, which began in 2001 after the adoption of Amendment 80 to the Constitution. Championed by then-Chief Justice Jim Hannah, it allowed the Supreme Court to select the time and place of oral arguments as opposed to just having them in Little Rock at the Justice Building. During my last years on the court, we held sessions from El Dorado to Jonesboro, from Fayetteville to Helena. This too demystified the court to people out in the state. After the arguments and conferences, we typically went to local high schools to address the students and answer questions.

Certainly many of the issues we dealt with when I was on the court were inflammatory. Once we were told to begin changing our route going home for security reasons. There was also the occasional threat to a justice, which we turned over to the State Police. There was also the execution in Arkansas of Richard Snell, who was with the white supremacist group, The Covenant, the Sword, and the Arm of the Lord. His execution occurred twelve hours before Timothy McVeigh blew up the Murrah Federal Building in Oklahoma City on April 19, 1995. That was no coincidence. We closed the Supreme Court courthouse that afternoon out of an abundance of caution.

What else undermines the public confidence? Certainly a judge or justice announcing views on an issue likely to come before that court is one of the most egregious examples. What leads to many claims of prejudgment are questionnaires sent out by special interest groups during judicial campaigns on controversial issues. I did not answer questionnaires in later elections because I was unopposed and did not feel the need to do so. But when asked my views on a certain "hot potato" issue during a public event, I would follow Justice Ginsburg's advice. I would not answer, because if that issue came before my court, I would be forced to recuse. People understood that. Tell the people the truth, as Harry Truman advised Dale Bumpers, and they can handle it.

CHAPTER 25

More Than Just a Lawyer – a Writer

In 1988, I was interviewed for one of the first High Profile features for the Sunday *Arkansas Democrat*. I told the interviewer I had always aspired to be more than just a lawyer, and there were some who thought I was disparaging my fellow attorneys. Not so. What I wanted was to do more with my law license than simply practice law. And I have.

Writing articles, working in Washington, running for the Supreme Court, and being elected are at the top of that list of achievements outside of practicing law. But a word about my writing. My paramount writing achievement has been *Defining Moments: Historic Decisions by Arkansas Governors from McMath through Huckabee*, published by the University of Arkansas Press in 2010 (Photograph 21).

My approach to *Defining Moments* was a riff on John F. Kennedy's *Profiles in Courage*. Like Kennedy, I sought to analyze pivotal moments in the careers of public figures. In my case, it was ten recent Arkansas governors. How did those pivotal moments reveal the governors' characters? The different moments soared with Winthrop Rockefeller's tribute to Martin Luther King on the Arkansas State Capitol steps in 1968 following the assassination, and plunged with Orval Faubus's calculated decision to call out the state militia to block integration at Central High. Through my research, I continued to be impressed by the caliber of men Arkansas had attracted to the governor's position. For the most part, the ten men profiled served honorably in the position and gained national recognition in the process. In that regard, we have been blessed.

My second major writing achievement was an analysis of the Little Rock School System thirty years after the Central High Crisis in 1957-58. The public policy project was entitled *The Second Crisis of Little Rock, A Report on Desegregation Within the Little Rock Public Schools* (Photograph 22).

The study was commissioned by the Winthrop Rockefeller Foundation, whose executive director at the time was my old friend from the Dale Bumpers gubernatorial days – Tom McRae. What had happened for better or worse since *Brown v. Board of Education*, the "troubles" at Central High, and the closing of the high schools in 1958-59? That was the question. My answer was "not enough." I interviewed forty-plus people for the report – from Hillary Clinton to school board presidents, to NAACP Legal Defense Fund counsel, to chamber of commerce presidents. The report was released in June 1988 and well received for raising complex, perhaps insurmountable issues.

At the time the report was written, Little Rock was conducting another experiment in public school assignments to have meaningful integration. The goal was desegregation while being ever mindful of white flight and the threat of a diminishing pool of white students from which to draw a racial balance. The hovering threat was with too few whites in a particular school, that school would reach a "tipping point," where whites would leave and the school would become all Black.

The report made the following recommendations directed primarily to the school boards and school administrations but also to the business community:

- There must be an unequivocal commitment to desegregated education.
- There must be a renewed effort to recruit more Black principals and teachers into Little Rock schools.

- Business involvement in the schools must increase with white business leaders supporting the public schools not only with their money but with the enrollment of their children and grand-children.
- Jobs and a college education should be available as incentives for disadvantaged children to complete their high school training.
- More effort is needed to bridge the social gap between the Black and white communities.
- Affordable housing for both races should be included in new developments in (the more affluent areas of) west Little Rock and west Pulaski County.
- The school administration must cease to have an us-against-them attitude toward segments of the community. Successes within the district need to be marketed. Better systems and personnel are needed to implement the goals and programs of the district.
- School board members must coalesce and remember that they represent the entire school district in addition to their individual zones.
- Serious effort must be made to remove the school district from federal court jurisdiction.
- The parties in the current litigation should agree to a morato-rium on desegregation litigation for six years. (This was to have a breather from court where headway could be made apart from litigation.)

That was more than thirty years ago. The sad truth is that my report is, in many respects, just as relevant today. No doubt strides have been made, especially in school funding (see *Lake* View). But curing the cancer of systematic racism is still very much a work in progress.

* * *

As already mentioned, throughout my professional life and while I was on the court and afterward, I wrote articles for a variety of publica-tions. The impetus for my writing career was simple. I had a compulsion to stay involved with the issues of the day and current events. Part of it was ego, but I also knew that advocating important changes like streaming oral arguments at the Supreme Court or providing judicial election reform were vitally important.

All told I published upward of thirty articles on non-legal subjects and an equal number of legal observations. There were also op-ed pieces that I routinely did on a variety of subjects. It has always been an enjoyable hobby and much like a second career. It kept me in the public eye and at times made a difference. My early articles about the pejorative impact of dark or hidden money pouring into layered corporations from out of state to influence judicial elections were notable for bringing attention to the problem.

My articles also occasionally inspired bitter responses. For example, I wrote in a piece championing prison reform that prosecutors like to get long sentences for their defendants and added I knew that because I had prosecuted cases myself. A prosecutor and a circuit judge took umbrage with my article. Both wrote that prosecutors did not work to get long sentences for their prey. Of course, their conclusions did not pass the laugh test. The job of the prosecutor is to prosecute and pursue convictions and statutory sentences. They are advocates. The jury then decides guilt, and the judge assesses the appropriate sentence. Prosecutors are not judges.

There also were disputes with members of the media. Sometimes an editorial writer, even the best, can get it wrong. The press is protected from government restraint by the First Amendment, as it should be. But public servants who are victims of erroneous and inflammatory editorial attacks are a different matter.

The conventional wisdom is never pick a fight with a newspaper editor because, as Mark Twain quipped, "He has ink by the barrel and paper by the ton." Yet when you are unfairly attacked with a misstatement of facts on the editorial page, and words like "disgraceful" and "hypocritical" are used against you, it is difficult to sit idly by and turn the other cheek. During my time on the court, I would respond to erroneous editorial attacks. Federal Judge Billy Roy Wilson often said he never lost a name-calling contest. At times one had to respond to unfair vilification.

My concluding thoughts about editorial writers is that the good ones mount cogent and well-reasoned arguments. The less able resort to erroneous statements, and vicious divisiveness.

* * *

One of the true benefits of being a justice was the summer break from roughly July 4 to the last week of August. Almost two months. At first, I did not know what to do with myself, but then I settled on a project. Why not travel and write the Great American Novel? Why not indeed?

It seemed like a capital idea to me. Charlotte was generously all on board with my taking this creative time away, and Stuart would be enjoying summer camp. I contacted good friend and Poe travel agent Nancy Dickins to help me. I took three solo trips for a month each to San Miguel d' Allende, Mexico; Oxford, England; and the country of Guatemala. All the adventures were just magnificent. I did write the Great American Novel about my days as a prosecuting attorney and one case in particular. It was Grisham-esk, and perhaps it will be my next book project.

* * *

I also wrote a play about Johnswood. Since buying the house, our mission has been to preserve the memory of the two writers who built it, wrote there, and eventually died there – John Gould Fletcher and Charlie May Simon (Photograph 23). The single-story home was designed by Maximilian F. (Max) Mayer and built in 1941, and we applied and it was listed on the National Register of Historic Places in 1994.

John committed suicide by drowning in a pond just off his land in 1951. He always suffered from bouts of depression. No doubt he was bipolar. After his death, Charlie May wrote *Johnswood*, a beautiful recount of the almost ten years they lived in Johnswood. I had been entranced by the Fletchers' story since college.

When Charlotte and I got the call about Charlie May's death from John Haley in 1976, we flew down from Washington to walk through the house. Charlotte often remarks that it was just like Charlie May had gone to the store. All of her clothes and personal items were still there. Charlotte was somewhat tentative at first about buying the house, but when she saw its potential she was all in. Now, if anything, she is a more fervent supporter and believer in the Fletcher-Simon legacy than I am.

And so we bought the five acres with the house and never looked back. Our relationship with Johnswood has been a romance. There have been school children who would come to the house on field trips, fans of the two authors' books who wanted to see where they wrote, and scholars who were studying their works. Lawyer and Little Rock legend Archie House arrived one day with his arms full of Fletcher first editions, dutifully autographed. He knew of our efforts to have all their books back on the Johnswood shelves and that many were out of print.

After we bought Johnswood in 1978 and had lived there several years, I wrote a play about John's and Charlie May's life together. At a benefit for the Arkansas Arts Center, now the Arkansas Museum of Fine Arts, Jackye and Curtis Finch purchased an event at our home that we decided to call "Evening at Johnswood."

The play was presented for the first time on our back terrace, which overlooks the woods and a vista view of the Arkansas River. Drinks and country supper buffet were included for the forty guests. Caroline Pugh, who had been with the Royal Shakespeare Company, and Bill Bond portrayed the couple. They sat on tall stools and recounted the life of John and Charlie May by quoting from their poetry, essays, and books.

Later, we added Starr Mitchell on the dulcimer and George West on the fiddle ("Lark in the Morning") to provide the background music. We have "produced" it many times over the years for friends and non-profit groups. Accomplished actors like Leslie Golden, Ruth Shepherd, Wayne Chapman, and Bill Jones continued to bring the Fletchers to life.

The play concludes with a quote from Charlie May's book where she describes waking to find John had gone:

> That night I slept soundly. All the worries and the tenseness and the endless hours of other nights I'd lain awake were lost completely in oblivion now. Even when I awoke the next morning at six, my regular time, I was still sleepy. I would have slept on, if I could, for days and weeks. I looked to see John still sleeping, too, and I wouldn't wake him. I'd drowse a little longer, I thought, and when I heard him stir, I'd get up and give him his morning medicine. I closed my eyes and knew nothing more until seven. And by then, John had dressed and was gone, driven by that urge that had haunted him his whole life long. (Simon, *Johnswood*, pp 234-5, EP Dutton 1953)

Probably the most memorable presentation of the play came after Charlotte had "rolled" son Stuart's 4Runner SUV three times on a rainy afternoon at the curve where Cantrell Road meets La Harpe Boulevard in Little Rock. She careened into the railing bordering the bridge overlooking the Union Pacific train tracks. There, but for the grace of God, she would have plunged to her death. She was rushing to a two-day symposium on John Gould Fletcher sponsored by the Central Arkansas Library System (CALS).

After the wreck and two plus hours in the hospital ER, she was released with only bad bruises to her ribs. She arrived at Johnswood just before the evening play and the supper reception that we were jointly hosting with CALS and the Butler Center for the symposium guests. I noticed her wince when tightly hugged by some of the grande dames in attendance, but at her insistence, no one had a clue about what had just transpired.

CHAPTER 26

Mercy and Justice – the
Quest Continues

After twenty-two years on the court I knew it was time to call a halt, which I did, effective January 1, 2013, just six months shy of my 72nd birthday. My real fear was that the job was becoming too routine and that I was doing the work by rote. Friend Walter Hussman maintains that at age 72 you begin to lose some of your professional acumen and that it is time for a CEO to turn the reins over to the next generation. I concur and believe the same applies to judging. Plus, the court needed new blood and a different lens through which to view the cases.

So I abandoned the court and in my final press release quoted from John Milton's poem "Lycidas" about the death of his young friend. It was time, he knew, to put the death behind him. He wrote: "Tomorrow to fresh woods and pastures new."

That is how I viewed it. Retirement became a fresh start for me. My roadmap was the old saw about what one does in retirement. You need a hobby (writing, a sport), a charity to support, and a project to assure intellectual stimulus. My base of operation became the Friday Law Firm where I am "of counsel."

In June 2012, Charlotte retired after serving nine years as development director at the Reynolds Institute on Aging at the University of Arkansas for Medical Sciences (UAMS). She had successfully worked in that same capacity at the Arkansas Arts Center (now the Arkansas Museum of Fine Arts) from 1991 to 2000 alongside executive director and chief curator Townsend Wolfe. Major capital campaigns for renovation and expansion were directed under her focused leadership at both of these leading institutions. During her two tenures she raised the impressive sum of $39 million dollars.

St. Margaret's Episcopal Church benefited from her fundraising prowess when she chaired its $1.2 million campaign to retire their church debt. She then joined hands with the Rev. Susan Sims Smith to secure $1 million to build the beautiful and architecturally acclaimed Arkansas House of Prayer located on the St. Margaret's grounds and served on its board for thirteen years. She is proudly referred to in our family as "The Builder."

Not wanting to go from full tilt to zero after retirement, Charlotte joined the boards of the Arkansas Museum of Fine Arts and the Arkansas Community Foundation and particularly enjoyed a volunteer stint through her membership in the Little Rock Garden Club with the Garden Club of America. She leads a full and busy life.

In my case, I "also boarded up," as Charlotte laughingly puts it, with multiple nonprofit opportunities that sprouted: the UAMS Board of Advisers; Central Arkansas Library System (CALS) Board; Winthrop Rockefeller Distinguished Lecture Series Committee, which I now chair; the Pathway to Freedom Board for inmate reentry; and the Highlands Cashiers Chamber Music Festival Board. It all keeps me engaged.

Writing op-ed pieces for the *Democrat-Gazette* continues to be a focus on old subjects like selection of justices and the corruption of money, but I also enjoy newer topics like the recidivism rate for released inmates, Winthrop Rockefeller's legacy in Arkansas, Arkansas poets, and the need for more women as our leaders.

In 1966 my parents bought a home in Cashiers, North Carolina, which is located in the western part of the state in the Blue Ridge Mountains. My sister, Wickie Plant, named the house "High Miter" after the headdress worn by bishops. It borders a small lake and is part of the High Hampton Club. My son Stuart calls High Miter his happy place and his wife, Victoria, and Annabel and Banks agree, especially Banks because there are fish in the lake. It has become our serene second home and we now live there six months out of the year. (Max Brantley of the *Arkansas Times* once referred to it as my dacha.).

It is our magnificent family who are our true pride and joy. Happily, they are not too far away and live in Dallas. In addition to their exceptional parenting skills, Stuart and Victoria are quite accomplished and successful in their chosen fields (Photograph 24). Stuart, a University of the South (Sewanee) and Wake Forest Business School graduate, is the founder and managing partner of HamptonRock Partners, which is an investment bank that advises companies on mergers and acquisitions and raising capital. Following in the family tradition, he was recently elected to the vestry, the managing board of St. Michael and All Angels Episcopal Church.

Armed with a master's degree in public affairs from the University of Texas in Austin, Victoria has dedicated herself and her career bridging multiple sectors to build a healthier America – no mean feat – and with a particular focus to help children and their families live longer, healthier lives. Working with the business communities across the country, she has tackled childhood obesity and the lack of nutritional value in our fast-food industry. After five years as senior program officer with the Robert Woods Johnson Foundation (RWF), she became a principal at Elemental Advisers. She and their talented coast-to-coast team work to transform organizations and counsel leaders at the highest levels of the non-profit, corporate and political sector to ensure organizations discern trends from fads to create positive social impact.

Granddaughter Annabel, age 14, is a tireless reader, excellent student, and deep thinker. She has a passion for modern dance and yearns for roles in Broadway musicals. Grandson Banks, age 12, is usually the fastest boy on the field, regardless of the sport, but he favors football with pads and lacrosse. He is also a pure shooter in basketball (Photograph 25).

What an exciting life they all have. My cup runneth over.

My two sisters live on opposite coasts. Wickie and her Renaissance man of a husband, Mac, live at Blakehurst, a retirement community in Baltimore. Kathy with her husband, Hollis Williams, who is a retired Episcopal minister, live in Seattle. I regretfully don't see either family enough, especially with the pandemic, but I intend to rectify that.

What's next for me? Probably dusting off that novel on my closet shelf.

* * *

Serving on the court for twenty-one years gave me a unique perspective of the human condition and a devoted respect for the law. I learned by experience to live Micah's admonition to do justice, love mercy, and walk humbly with my God. There was a wholeness that came from this understanding and a satisfaction that my life had been guided in this direction. To me, administering justice with an eye toward mercy was the ultimate fulfillment, and I am thankful that my career culminated with this achievement.

ACKNOWLEDGMENTS

A book, like a ruling from a court, is the product of many minds working together behind the scenes, and I am grateful to all who contributed to this work. My wife, Charlotte, of course, was invaluable in reading and re-reading the manuscript, not only improving the writing but also helping to fill some the gaps in my memory. Stephen Caldwell came recommended to me as a content editor, and he smoothed out some rough edges and challenged me to add greater detail in telling my story. My good friend Julie Keller policed my grammar and was essential to the process because of her sharp editorial eye. I'm also thankful to Cindy Momchilov at Camera Work Photos for her assistance with the photographs in the book and to Hunter Gray for his design of the front and back covers, including his placement of quotes from the manuscript and from readers. Many others shaped this book simply by being part of my life – the many friends, co-workers, and family members who show up in the pages. There are too many to thank by name in print, but rest assured all of you have the deepest gratitude in my heart.

About the Author

Robert (Bob) Brown turned a lifelong love of law, literature, and politics into a career in public service that culminated with twenty-one years as an associated justice of the Arkansas Supreme Court.

As the son of an Episcopal priest, Brown's family moved from Texas to Virginia to Arkansas, where his father was elected bishop just in time for the Central High School desegregation crisis in Little Rock. Brown graduated magna cum laude and was a member of Phi Beta Kappa with a degree in English literature from Sewanee, the University of the South, in Tennessee, then earned a master's degree in English and comparative literature from Columbia University and a juris doctorate from the University of Virginia.

He and Charlotte (Banks) of Fordyce married in 1966 and, after he completed law school, returned to Arkansas, where he briefly practiced law before getting involved in politics. Brown did precinct work for Winthrop Rockefeller in his 1968 campaign for governor and served on the staffs of Dale Bumpers (as governor and a United States senator) and Jim Guy Tucker (as prosecuting attorney and a United States congressman).

He was elected to the Arkansas Supreme Court in 1991 and authored several opinions that shaped the landscape of the state's history, including the Lake View desegregation case and a pivotal case on term limits. Along the way, he also authored books and articles for legal journals, newspapers, and magazines.

CPSIA information can be obtained
at www.ICGtesting.com
Printed in the USA
LVHW050913090622
720770LV00015B/1315